THE SAGA
OF RED RYAN

THE SAGA
OF RED RYAN

AND OTHER
TALES OF VIOLENCE
FROM CANADA'S PAST

MARTIN ROBIN

Western Producer Prairie Books
Saskatoon, Saskatchewan

Cover design by Warren Clark/GDL

Western Producer Prairie Books publications are produced and manufactured in the middle of western Canada by a unique publishing venture owned by a group of prairie farmers who are members of Saskatchewan Wheat Pool. From the first book in 1954, a reprint of a serial originally carried in the weekly newspaper, *The Western Producer*, to the book before you now, the tradition of providing enjoyable and informative reading for all Canadians is continued.

Canadian Cataloguing in Publication Data

Robin, Martin, 1936-
    The saga of Red Ryan and other tales of
violence from Canada's past

    Includes index.
    ISBN 0-88833-098-7

    1. Crime and criminals — Canada — Biography.
I. Title.
HV6805.R62   364.1'092'2   C82-091326-X

To my daughters,
Sarah and Mira

CONTENTS

PREFACE

This book is about neither Inheritors nor Acquisitors. Its principals inherited little and, with the exception of His Lordship during his high-flying days, acquired even less. Nor does virtue notably abound among these gentlemen, whose lives were rich mainly in drama, tribulation, and, in most instances, pathos.

The stories recounted here are drawn from the real historical record and are based on research into a variety of primary and secondary sources. I thank the many persons — librarians, researchers, Simon Fraser University secretarial staff, my publisher and editors — who helped along the way. My wife, Grace, encouraged and supported the project from beginning to end, and I thank her.

1
HIS LORDSHIP

It was a hot, mosquito-infested evening in Winnipeg, and the excitement of Dominion Day, 1873, had cleanly evaporated into the parched air of the prairie summer. The fun was over. The cricketers were gone, tired horses munched hay in their stables, Caledonian athletes nursed pulled groins and sore hamstrings, while the rustic crowds rested in their homes, scattered along the dirt roads and ruts of Lower and Upper Fort Garry. At Silver Heights, on the porch of the Honourable James McKay's residence, Buckhorn's Lodge, a lone gentleman leaned back in his chair, his feet resting on the wooden rail, and gazed out pensively at the moonlit prairie.

The lolling gentleman was in his late forties, of medium height, slim build, with a protuberant forehead, brown hair, straggly side-whiskers, and gray eyes. Usually nervous and restless, with "a peculiarly stiff and set way of holding his head up and back," he seemed, on this quiet evening, relaxed and inattentive to anything except the chirp of crickets and slow descent of dusk over the neighboring fields. Around eight o'clock in the evening, however, the gentleman's composure was ruffled by a pair of intruders who had arrived unnoticed at the rear of the house, in a wagon driven along a back road by a local livery-stable keeper. Armed with pistols and billies, the visitors stole up on their oblivious victim, pointed a pistol at his head, seized him bodily, and, amid shouts and screams, dragged him along the nearby road to the waiting wagon where he was shoved into the front seat alongside the driver. As the wagon, drawn by a pair of white-and-brown horses, lit out along the roadway south towards Pembina at the American border, McKay's captive guest was hauled into the back seat and bound and secured between his burly captors, a pair of policemen who, several days earlier, had been dispatched on their secret abduction mission from Minneapolis, Minnesota.

While the Americans knew they had the right man, they were not at

1

Lord Gordon Gordon circa 1870. Manitoba Archives

all certain of his correct name. He had, in fact, several identities that changed with time of day, style of wardrobe, or locale. In Winnipeg, he called himself Gordon Gordon or Gordon Harcourt Gordon. In Minneapolis and New York, where he dealt with Jay Cooke and Colonel Loomis of the Northern Pacific Railroad and earned the acrimony of Jay Gould, of Erie Railway fame, he was known as the Right Honourable Gordon H. Gordon or Lord Gordon Gordon. And back in England and Scotland, where his troubled life and odd ways had begun, he assumed the various names of John Hamilton, Hubert Hamilton, and, more elegantly, Lord Glencairn.

The odd trajectory of His Lordship's career began in the county of Kent, England where a local rector discovered one disconsolate day in the late 1830s, that his extramarital liaison with a young lady had brought forth into the world a bawling male infant. Named John Hamilton, the child was sent off at the age of two to a boarding school run by a Mrs. Berry of Colwich Common, where he apparently remained until his early youth. Young Hamilton's troubles started soon after his entry into the work world. While employed with Messrs. White and Sons, warehousemen, of Cheapside, London, he was arrested on a charge of obtaining goods under false pretenses but released after the prosecution failed to press its case.

Whatever quirk of character may have driven young John to pretense at Cheapside remained with him in subsequent years, in other places and employments. Indeed, pretense, of a dramatic and serious sort, seemed to become the predominant trait of the foundling's adult personality. Two years after leaving his warehouse job, Hamilton turned up in the town of Yeovil in Somersetshire where, with scant training but plausible intelligence, he performed as an assistant master at a school. Not content with this lowly vocation, he adopted the role of a man of wealth, befriended local gentlemen, obtained credit here and there, and absconded "without recollecting to settle his 'little bills.' "

Somersetshire's little bills grew in London, Edinburgh, and sundry other places to large denominations. And the Yeovil poses took on finer forms and new dimensions. Fond of the sacerdotal office, Hamilton presided for a while at a church in London, until the cloth was removed and his deceit exposed. He appeared next at Surbiton and Orchard Court Hook, adopted the christian name of Hubert, hinted at a lordship, and divided a good part of his time between two ladies — a Miss Bayley, who was introduced around as his bride-to-be, and a Mrs. Sarah Berry, whom he resided with in an elegantly furnished house and passed off as an aunt, until she died. Hamilton then sold the furniture and made for London where, in 1886, he earned the confidence of a prominent attorney, Mr. Howard Paddison of Number 57, Lincoln's Inn Fields, London.

3

Paddison was fond of his new client, took care of some legal matters, extended him credit, accepted assorted gifts of jewelry, and willingly postponed collection of legal fees. When Hamilton intimated that he was a member of the Cunningham family, heir to the earl of Glencairn, and would come into vast fortunes and estates upon resumption of the title in late March, 1870, Paddison bought his story. Prior to his departure north to Scotland during the summer of 1868, in search of game, human and animal, Hamilton left in Paddison's care several japanned tin boxes bearing the gold lettering "The Right Honourable Lord Glencairn" containing, presumably, valuable jewels, deeds, titles, and other lordly possessions.

At Glenisla in the county of Forfarshire, Scotland, John Hamilton rented a shooting box and impressed the local citizenry with his erect but nervous bearing, his arched back, elocution, manners, pedigree, and retinue. An elderly farmer he had known for some time, a Mr. Bird, was introduced as his steward, while a young boy dressed in top boots, buckskin breeches, and a hat-cockade, served as the "gentleman's tiger." Hamilton deposited £1,000 at the City of Glasgow Bank, Dundee; established a line of credit; lived quietly; bagged birds; and on Sundays attended the Free Church Manse at Glenisla, officiated over by the Reverend J. W. Simpson. The Reverend, like Mr. Paddison, who joined His Imminent Lordship for the 1869 shoot, was taken with, if not by, Hamilton. He bought his story about the properties in Ayrshire, Lancashire, and Northamptonshire; the imminent resumption of the earldom of Glencairn; the coming Birthday Ball; the vast sums tied up in chancery pending legal settlement. When Lord Glencairn, as he now called himself, hinted about an introduction to a prominent firm of Edinburgh tradesmen, the Reverend gladly complied and brought "a man of gentlemanly appearance and deportment" around for a meeting with the carriage-trade goldsmiths, Marshall and Sons, of Number 87, George Street, Edinburgh.

Marshall and Sons were ready to do business with Glencairn after first checking out his claims in the Book of Scottish Peerage, which they consulted in their store almost daily. In it, they found that the title of the earl of Glencairn had been dormant since 1796, "upon the death of John, fifteenth Earl of Glencairn," and that the Cunningham family was one of the two claimants to the title. The Marshall and Sons people assumed, as their spokesman later claimed, "that Glencairn belonged to some branch of the Cunningham family, the family of the Earl of Glencairn, and was what he claimed to be ... without enquiring into the precise nature and origin of his claims, by questions which, both his introduction, his manner, and his supposed rank, seemed to forbid."

Lord Hubert Glencairn, socially and conversationally, was forthcoming. He visited the goldsmiths regularly and entertained his hosts with innumerable stories of noble personages, including his late cousin, the marquis of Hastings; his relative, the duke of Hamilton; and his good friend, the Prince of Wales. He talked occasionally about his mother, "a very gay lady," and his father whom he held in the highest regard. One day, he casually recalled, for the entertainment of Mr. Thomas Smith, a partner in Marshall and Sons, a telling incident. "I will tell you what transpired, one day when I was your eldest boy's age; at breakfast time my father called me into his room and said to me, 'Hubert, you have now come to that time of life when you're going to enter into the world; you know how bright your prospects are; deny yourself nothing; whatever your taste or inclination leads you to, gratify; but never do anything that you would not like me to know. . . .' "

In his dealings with Marshall and Sons, as with other firms, there was a decent measure of give-and-take. Sometimes His Lordship gave. "He . . . told us one day, in conversation," Mr. Smith recalled, "that he was possessed of a porcelain portrait of the mother of the first Napoleon; that it had reached the knowledge of the ex-emperor Napoleon of France; that he was possessed of this portrait; and the Emperor wrote to him that he would like to see it; that he prized it so highly that he would not risk it by sending it to the Tuileries, but that he sent a special messenger with it, with strict orders that it was not to be let out of his hands; that the Emperor subsequently offered him £10,000 to become possessed of it, and he refused the offer." What Glencairn denied Napoleon, he gave to Marshall and Sons, "on show," for a short time. For a brief few days, the Glencairn Napoleonic porcelain, whatever its true origin or worth, was displayed in the window, after arrival from London in a brown paper wrapper addressed to "The Right Honourable H. Glencairn, Royal Hotel, Edinburgh."

But His Lordship much preferred taking to giving, and during months of business with Marshall and Sons he took, on credit, a sizable collection of exquisite items. During each of his many visits to Edinburgh, he dropped in on the firm for hours at a time. "He declared himself a connoisseur in such articles as we manufactured and sold, and was very particular regarding those made for him," Smith recalled; "he often had the foreman called in and sketched the articles he desired, and wrote down minute directions for guidance." The take piled up: oval gold lockets studded with rubies, diamonds, and emeralds; buhl vases; fine gold rings embellished with three brilliants; silver-mounted knives; a goatskin sporran mounted with silver and engraved; brooches, teapots, muffiners, sugar tongs, toddy ladels, studs, pins, flasks, buckles, and more.

Glencairn did not keep all of the take; or take all of it to keep. Some items found their way into the lordly trove, while others were passed on as gifts to friends and acquaintances whose business and confidence he sought. What Glencairn did with, or to, Marshall and Sons, he repeated with other firms: bankers in Rugby and Dundee, hosiery merchants, jewelers, and assorted tradesmen in Edinburgh, London, and elsewhere.

The take was easy, until early in the year 1870, when a nervous, erect gentleman, calling himself Lord Glencairn of Auchinleith, Perthshire, arrived at the door of Mr. L. Kellers, diamond merchant, at Number 88, Hatton Garden, in the city of London. While Mr. Kellers lent some weight to a referral from Mr. Paddison, he remained suspicious enough of the noble supplicant to send off a letter of inquiry about him to Marshall and Sons, old associates, Glencairn claimed, with whom he had done business for years. When Mr. Smith received the Kellers letter, he strongly suspected a hoax, telegraphed Kellers to detain Glencairn should he appear, took a train to London, compared notes, and concluded he had been duped. He then headed for Paddison's Lincoln's Court office, which Glencairn used as his London business address.

Mr. Paddison proved testy and difficult when Smith arrived at his door and intimated that His Lordship was not around. But when Smith pressed the matter, after observing a pile of Forfarshire game on the floor, a Scottish toque on a table, and a "gentleman's tiger" peeping through an adjoining doorway, he relented and led Smith up a landing and flight of stairs into a well-appointed room, announced as His Lordship's "audience chamber." His Lordship was home, seated elegantly at a writing table among fine carpets, decorous chairs, a tasteful ottoman, a smattering of gold-embossed and calf-bound books, and, on the walls, several maps laid out to show His Imminent Lordship's imminent estates. Glencairn was friendly enough and exchanged general pleasantries with Mr. Smith, acknowledging that he well understood that gentleman's concerns. But he referred all business matters to his solicitor, who soon offered to return forthwith the goods still in Glencairn's possession and deliver up a check for the residue. "At the same time," Smith later disclosed, "he said that if we did that, it would be very foolish for our interest, as His Lordship intended to make very extensive purchases in jewellery, to give away to various parties, and that he had been very much satisfied with the way we conducted ourselves." Smith hesitated, thought about the matter further, and when Paddison offered a written personal guarantee that the debts would be paid by March 25, he relented and returned home to Edinburgh.

By late March, 1870, the month of the lordly assumption, there was only one new development of any consequence — H. Glencairn's disappearance. After borrowing £800 from his solicitor-benefactor and bringing his total indebtedness to him to £5,000, he vacated his audience chamber and announced that he was going north to collect rents and arrears. When he failed to appear at the end of the month, Paddison panicked and sent a clerk to look for him. Mr. Smith, in the meanwhile, took a train to London and presented himself at Paddison's doorstep, guarantee in hand. He found Paddison distraught and convinced that he had been duped. Smith made the most of a bad deal and accepted in settlement various valuable items made by his firm, amounting to two-thirds of the claims owed, which Glencairn had presented as gifts to the Paddison family during the past months. Similar Glencairn gifts, from employees of the Old Rugby and Dundee bankers, who suffered losses of their own, trickled back in subsequent weeks as Marshall and Sons exchanged condolences with other duped tradesmen: Messrs. Cruickshank and Sons, Romanes and Paterson, McRae and Shand, Grant and Peake, and others. Although bilked of £5,000, apart from legal fees unpaid, and nearly ruined, Howard Paddison had this one consolation. He was not alone.

While Glencairn's dupes tallied their losses, His Lordship managed to place himself at a safe distance. More than a year after his hurried departure, in August or September of 1871, a strange gentleman materialized in and around Minneapolis, Minnesota, a rustic city of 20,000 in the west of the United States of America. "This extraordinary tourist was a man of impressive appearance," a local journalist observed: "he was slender of build, about five feet ten inches in height, and dressed with the greatest care, usually wearing gloves, patent leathers, and a silk hat. His hands were frequently manicured, and his hair was brushed as smooth as curly hair could be. He was clean-shaven, except for two tufts of side whiskers, à l'Anglaise. He was exceedingly self poised . . . and deliberate of speech, articulated with much precision, and posed with an amount of ceremony seldom seen on the American continent."

Amidst Minnesota's rubes, His Lordship, The Right Honourable George Herbert Gordon — or Lord Gordon Gordon, as he called himself — stood out like a piece of fine porcelain or golden toddy spoon. He parked himself at a local hotel, collected and dispatched letters adorned with the monogram GHG and an earl's coronet, spent lavishly, deposited a large amount of money in William H. Westfall's National Exchange Bank, and talked here and there, with great effect, about affinities with the great earls of Gordon, consanguinity with the Aberdeens, collateral relations with Lord Byron, bilateral ties with the marquises of Cunningham and Huntly, and descent from the bold Lochinvar and ancient highland kings.

The rubes' eyebrows rose, and His Lordship soon picked and chose among invitations to banquets and luncheons and shoots, where he

7

outlined the moral purpose of his frontier visit. "Yes, I do covet a few thousand acres of your beautiful lands," the *Minneapolis Tribune* one day quoted him, "not for myself — I have more than enough for the remnant of my poor life — but for my beloved sister, for the gratification of her benevolence. She would like to present to some of my old tenants lands in your free Republic where they may rear their families in peace and plenty; and, to gratify my beautiful sister, I would like to buy a few thousand acres — not many thousand, you know — say — say — say — say — about — about fifty thousand or so — just a little for my poor people."

In playing Lord Selkirk, His Lordship found willing ears among officials of the Northern Pacific Railway Company, which owned huge tracts of land throughout the state of Minnesota. Long on scandal and short on cash, the Northern Pacific people wined and dined their noble guest who, it was rumored, was one of the great monied men of Europe and possessed of an annual income of £235,000. The wife of the railway's president, Mrs. Jay Cooke, who warmed to his boudoir style, presented His Lordship with several lovely pieces of silver, while Col. John J. Loomis, the railway's land commissioner, arranged for an excursion through the railway lands to better help His Lordship pick and choose.

The Gordon expedition was a lavish and widely advertised affair that lasted for several months and wandered through a vast territory, including Fergus Falls, Moorehead, Detroit Lake, Oak Lake, and Pelican Rapids. Colonel Loomis himself attended for part of the trip, together with his personal secretary, his attorney, and a pair of surveyors on horseback, playfully referred to as "land tasters," who pointed out choice portions of real estate. The caravan included an entire wagon to carry hunting equipment and a second car for fishing gear. Lord Gordon slept and supped in a large wall tent adorned at one end with the Stars and Stripes, and at the other, with a peculiar flag, of vague historic import, referred to as "His Lordship's flag." "Can the glories of that caravan be told?" the *Minneapolis Tribune* expostulated; "there were half a dozen teams with a carriage for Milord, beside the omnibuses, ambulances, etc. There were twelve men to do the manual labor, and a French cook and darky waiters in linen aprons and white silk gloves, and the royal table was unloaded from the baggage wagons at every meal, and set out with fresh napkins, silver-plate, and china . . . every luxury that the markets of Chicago, Saint Paul and Minneapolis could provide was there and all the game of the boundless prairie, from woodcock to buffalo. Champagne three times a day. When the caravan had skirted Oak Lake, Milord wanted to see Fergus Falls, and when it had done Fergus Falls, he longed for Moorehead, and when it had digested Moorehead, he yearned to visit the glimpses of the moon beyond the Red River."

Colonel Loomis invested more than twenty thousand dollars of Northern Pacific cash in the famed Gordon expedition, but no quick results followed. Reports of imminent land sales totaling thirty to forty thousand acres, of delicate negotiations, of international money transfers, of model towns peopled by immigrant crofters leaked and dribbled into the Minneapolis and Saint Paul press, as His Lordship pondered landscapes, blueprints, and counties. But nothing happened except the formation of some sort of partnership with a William H. Tuttle, who owned acreage around Pelican Rapids where the new town of Loomis, named after the Northern Pacific Railway commissioner, was destined to rise. On Gordon's assurance that funds would be available for schools and other facilities to house and service his poor people, Mr. Tuttle employed surveyors, laborers, and mechanics to plot the land and build a mill dam, half of which was completed when it was discovered that the land from which the trees were cut still belonged to the railway. A large stumpage fee was exacted and Mr. Tuttle went under.

By Christmas, 1872, Lord Gordon Gordon had tired of land play with Minnesota's rubes and prepared for a grander game, at the very citadel of gilded America: Wall Street, New York City. The instrument of His Lordship's deliverance from the Twin Cities was Mrs. Loomis, who one day introduced him to a Mrs. Patten, wife of a Colonel Patten of Poughkeepsie, and her son and daughter, the wife of the prominent financier William Belden.[1] When Mrs. Patten and her entourage left Saint Paul, they were joined by Gordon, who traveled with them as far as Milwaukee, then quietly disappeared. A day after their arrival in New York, however, Mr. Belden received a telegram announcing the residency of Gordon at the Westminster Hotel. His Lordship was soon at their door, stayed for several weeks, and entertained his hosts with windy accounts of his lordly doings. He spoke of his pedigree and possessions in Scotland. He talked of the large tract of Northern Pacific Railway land he had purchased and produced a map of a town named Loomis near Pelican Rapids, marked out with schools, houses, and churches, all, apparently, under construction. He expressed his hope that his projected wilderness city would be completed in time for the arrival of 500 Scottish immigrants in April. He informed his hosts of his entrance into the House of Lords at twenty-two or twenty-three years of age, the youngest peer on record, and repeated a portion of a speech once delivered to his

---

1. According to the *New York Times*, August 20, 1873, reproducing an article in the *Duluth Herald*, Gordon had filched from Mrs. Loomis a "magnificent solitaire diamond ring," which she had removed from her finger and placed on a washstand while staying at the Metropolitan Hotel in Saint Paul. Gordon pocketed the ring when he entered her room to pay respects and the diamond was later given up for lost.

fellow peers, who were so enthralled that a dropped pin could be distinctly heard in the House. According to Mrs. Belden, he often favored his hosts with the expression "We peers of the Realm" and reminded them of delicate negotiations he had once conducted with Bismarck on behalf of Her Majesty's government. Indeed, Gordon repeated, his services had been called upon whenever difficult matters of state needed settlement.

With skills like these, it is no wonder that His Lordship insinuated himself, in good time, into the very bosom of American finance capitalism. After leaving the Beldens, he set up in grand style at the Metropolitan Hotel on Broadway, run by Richard Tweed, the son of William H. Tweed, renowned boss of the Tammany Hall machine. From here, the Lord's aura and reputation diffused among the smoke-filled rooms and posh suites, including the gilded salon above Pike's Grand Opera Palace, where the affairs of the Scarlet Woman of American transportation, the Erie Railroad, were attended to.

Erie news was big news in New York state when Lord Gordon first rested his bewhiskered cheeks on the down pillows at Boss Tweed's Metropolitan. Begun in 1832, with trackage stretching from New York City to Buffalo and as far west as Chicago, the Erie had been plagued in recent years by widely advertised and bitter struggles between the incumbent regime, led by a slight tycoon with "dark, vulpine and acutely piercing eyes," Mr. Jay Gould, and hordes of insurgent stockholders, many of them from Britain, who had nearly drowned themselves in tankfuls of Erie's watered stock.

In taking on Gould, the rebels had their work cut out. Variously described by Mr. Gustavus Myers as "the most cold-blooded corruptionist, spoliator and financial pirate of his time," "a pitiless human carnivore," and "an incarnate fiend of a Machiavelli," Gould had learned a great deal about the arts of financial war during his rise from cattle droving in the backwoods of Roxbury, through "the swamp" of New York's tanning industry, and, finally, within the pitiless jungle of Wall Street and national railway politics. Erie was Jay Gould's big prize, the former drover's golden cow, which, according to Myers, he milked of $12,000,000. Along the way he bribed legislators, bought judges, seduced editors, played the crowds, and employed Tammany and thugs to beat back opposition to his thousand diversionary schemes.

When His Lordship first turned his noble attention to Wall Street, Jay Gould was under an unprecedentedly withering fire from insurgents, British and American, who had gathered in and around an informal organization known as the Erie Stockholders Protective Organization. Being a compassionate sort, Gordon decided to help Gould out. But he first studied and mastered the Erie situation and built up his credibility among the right people, including Mr. Horace Greeley, presidential candidate to be and editor of the influential *New York Tribune*. Since Gordon shared with Greeley an interest in immigration and western settlement and, as a brash young man, had even heeded his admonition to "Go West" to Minnesota, before rebounding east onto Wall Street, they became solid acquaintances. Like His Lordship's other friends, Greeley warmed to stories about the earldom, the properties, the railway lands, the Scottish crofters, the House of Lords, and all that. Most important of all, Greeley believed Lord Gordon Gordon when he spoke of owning and controlling a vast sum of Erie shares, which he was prepared to use for the betterment of that company's unhappy affairs.

Through Horace Greeley, Lord Gordon Gordon met other important personages on the high road to Jay Gould. Colonel A. K. McClure of the *Philadelphia Times* enjoyed his company and brought him into touch with Col. Thomas A. Scott, vice-president of the Pennsylvania Railway Company, who learned of Gordon's intention to include him among his projected new board of Erie directors.

It was over an omelette in His Lordship's suite at the Metropolitan Hotel, in the company of Greeley and Scott, that arrangements were made to bring Gordon to Gould or, more correctly, Gould to Gordon. When the telegram went out from Colonel Scott to "the Mephistopheles of Wall Street" suggesting that he drop in on Gordon at the Metropolitan, Gould jumped at the chance and, in the morning of March 2, 1872, appeared at his door.

The robber baron was treated to the Scottish lord's usual elaborations, though with quaint variations here and there. "He told me about his antecedents," Gould later swore, "his career and his family, stated that he entered Parliament at the age of twenty-two, and took his seat as the youngest member of the House of Lords; spoke of the great confidence the Queen had in his ability and his discretion, and mentioned delicate missions that had been entrusted to him — an important negotiation with the Prussian Government, which he was sent out to attend to as the only man who could cope with Bismarck." Jay Gould learned about His Lordship's sister, the baroness of Kurl in Italy; His Lordship's trustee, the count de Crano of Florence, who released "five hundred thousand or six hundred thousand pounds, on the attainment of his majority"; and His Lordship's escort, the Prince of Wales, who had accompanied him on an expedition across Canada a few years earlier. And the baron noted the gold pin attached to the lord's lapel, a gift from Bismarck, who had attempted to "euchre" him during one of several confidential missions conducted on behalf of Queen Victoria to the German court.

However diverting the tales, Gould was less interested in His Lordship's antecedents than in his assets and his position on Erie affairs.

11

"I asked him what his intent was," Gould recalled; "he said that individually he owned 30 millions of the stock; his friends, 20 millions more; that he was satisfied that it was best to keep the road under my management, but wanted to put in a new Board to be selected by himself and Horace Greeley — all the Gentlemen to be approved by me."

For an entire week, the baron and lord furiously sparred. Puts and calls were put and called, concentrated and diluted stock were poured over both of them, pledges and guarantees were tossed about like baseballs at Wrigley Field. Finally, a deal was struck, taking into account, of course, the lord's large monies expended on behalf of the Erie reform movement. "Gordon represented to Gould," wrote one student of the Gould-Gordon meetings, "that in making his investigations, and getting bills passed and bringing litigations to an end, he had been at a very large expense; that his bills had been paid by him personally."[2] When Gordon intimated that his investigations had cost $1,000,000, Gould offered relief and a tangible pledge of his own good faith. "In view of the fact that he made these advances personally," Gould later explained, "and that the success of the new plan would depend very much on my good faith and his co-operation, I agreed to deposit with him securities and money to the extent of about one-half of his expenses, or about $500,000. This pledge was not to be used by him, it was to be returned to me on my carrying out part of my agreement."

When Jay Gould finally delivered the goods to Gordon's Metropolitan suite, His Lordship checked out the footing, noted what he thought to be an error, and asked for a further $40,000 in cash. Gould obliged and when Gould requested a receipt for the securities and money, Gordon took the high ground that his word was sufficient and returned the entire parcel into Gould's arms. Gould was almost at the door when he reconsidered, returned the package, and accepted, in place of a memorandum of receipt, Lord Gordon Gordon's trusted word.

It was, without doubt, His Lordship's finest moment, the consummation of the master bluff of his career, the sublime moment of triumph of a bogus peer over a Yankee tycoon. Of the many dupes strewn along his path of pretense, from Cheapside, London to Wall Street, New York, none was as distinguished, or improbable, as the Mephistopheles of Wall Street. But Gordon's dazzling success seemed to have a narcotic and paralyzing effect, not merely on Mr. Gould, who recovered quickly enough, but on his own person. Instead of flying, by night or day, booty

---

2. Gordon represented that he had fought for the withdrawal of a Classification Act, passed earlier by the State Legislature to guarantee perpetuation of the incumbent leadership. The Classification Act provided for the re-election of a small minority of board members staggered over several years and prevented any wholesale change in membership.

in hand, to some far corner of the world, he lingered at the Metropolitan; maintained his pretenses, wardrobe, and suite; and quietly sold off some of Gould's shares. A few lots of the Erie stock were quietly dropped on the New York exchange, while a bundle of Oil Creek and Allegheny Valley shares were placed on the market in Philadelphia.

Of these, Mr. Jay Gould got wind. In the midst of his war with the Erie insurgents, Gould came to the astounding realization that he had been duped. He wasted no time in righting matters. In the company of some local notables, he occupied the chamber adjoining Gordon's at the Metropolitan. William Belden acted as the intermediary and, after knocking gently on His Lordship's door, gained admission and demanded restitution on Gould's behalf. According to one account, Gordon treated the demand with indifference, until Belden proved to him that Gould was in an adjoining room with William H. Tweed, late commissioner of public works, Chief of Police Kelso, and Judge Shandley and that he would immediately be locked up and all his papers seized. He then returned the whole of the money and securities with the exception of shares to the value of $35,000. Belden took them to the parties in the adjoining room and returned to Gordon, stating that Gould and Tweed were utterly surprised at their success and that Gould had given him $10,000 for his services. At the same time, he informed Gordon that "The Ring" were determined to get him out of the way, that it was not safe for him to remain in the hotel alone, and that it would not be the first time a person had suddenly disappeared or been "knocked out and disabled for life."

His Lordship was scared but not badly enough to cause him to surrender all or leave town immediately. When Jay Gould demanded, through his agent Belden, that Gordon write out and hand over orders to his Philadelphia brokers to halt the sale of some of the Oil Creek and Allegheny Valley shares, His Lordship complied. But after Gould left, he reversed himself and "directed his Philadelphia brokers not to hand over the order he had furnished to Gould and to deliver that stock to no one but himself." Gould was upset and launched an action in the Supreme Court of New York, alleging wrongful conversion of both the Oil Creek and Erie shares, which, he maintained, were not Gordon's to dispose of and had been obtained under false pretenses. Gordon was arrested on order of Supreme Court Judge John R. Brady and quickly bailed out for $37,000 by a pair of prominent enemies of Jay Gould, Mr. A. F. Roberts, a wealthy merchant, and Horace F. Clark, the millionaire son-in-law of Commodore Vanderbilt and president of the Union Pacific Railway, who left his bed at midnight to aid His Lordship in his hour of need.

In the days and weeks following His Lordship's release, the famous Gould-Gordon suit heated up. Gordon launched a counter action alleging that Gould had wrongfully dispossessed him of shares and cash. Prominent counsel lined up on both sides: David Dudley Field, Elihu Root, and General Charles H. T. Collis for Gould, and ex-judge John K. Porter and a Mr. John H. Strachan for Gordon. Contradictory affidavits were filed. Gould's vowed that he had been swindled by an imposter, while Gordon protested plain dealings and honest claims. He denied ever posing as the earl of Aberdeen, as a Scottish peer, or member of the British House of Lords and claimed that he had been brought up as Gordon Harcourt Gordon — his baptismal name — by his mother, who told him that his dead father, whom he had never known, had been a Scottish duke. Since, "as far back as recollection" extended, he had been addressed by his mother, his relations, and acquaintances as Lord Gordon Gordon or, for abbreviation, Lord Gordon, he thought nothing of continuing its use as a courtesy title which "he considered himself entitled to use as the younger son of a duke."

Lord Gordon's affidavit read beautifully; it flowed as smoothly as the soft words of his testament delivered during the trial's early hours. But when Gould's leading counsel, David Dudley Field, pressed for details on family matters, the flow slowed, and Gordon volunteered a string of fictitious names and addresses, placing his stepfather, a sister, a brother-in-law, and an uncle in several European cities. Field had what he wanted and, when the court adjourned, sent out cablegrams to American consulates in Paris, London, and Berne, to check out the names and addresses. When the hearing resumed on May 27, Field and his associates arrived in court fortified with a batch of negative replies and with fresh new evidence volunteered by Mr. Thomas Smith of Marshall and Sons, Edinburgh, whose suspicions, that Gordon was really Glencairn, were first roused by an account of the Gould-Gordon suit in the *Edinburgh Scotsman*. Through a friend in New York City, Smith was supplied with a full batch of press clippings about Gordon's New York operations. He drew the proper conclusions, collected pictures and documents relating to Lord Glencairn, and sailed for the New World.

Unfortunately for Mr. Smith, Lord Gordon was not around when he arrived. He was not even present in court when Mr. Field, acting for Gould, and Mr. Strachan, acting for Gordon, showed up for the resumption of the trial at the end of May. When urgent inquiries were made at the Metropolitan, it was disclosed that Gordon had left several days earlier, after an express wagon, and not the usual hotel conveyance, had arrived at the front door, loaded up, and taken off towards the train station. No forwarding address, for mail or summonses, had been left.

Lord Gordon Gordon's next stop was Toronto, Ontario, Canada, which he might well have reached with the aid of a complimentary Erie pass, courtesy of Jay Gould. Since no large scandals or swindles involving an outlaw lord hit the headlines of the Toronto dailies during his tenure there, it can safely be assumed that the stopover was brief. With Messrs. Thomas Smith, Elihu Root, and General Collis in pursuit, His Lordship vacated for Montreal, which he quickly tired of. Sometime in the early autumn of 1873, Lord Gordon left Montreal and took a long, painful route westward by train, steamer, and wagon, across 1,500 miles of blue lakes, pine forest, and pre-Cambrian rock, to "a muddy, generally disreputable village," bounded by "prairie to the right, prairie to the left" and prairie in front and rear.

In Winnipeg, Manitoba, perched at the southeast periphery of the Great Lone Land, His Lordship found an "infantile and arcadian community," living close to the land and suitably distant from the bustle, vices, and law courts, of the Old World. In its culture and amenities, Manitoba's capital was a far cry from New York City, Edinburgh, or even Glenisla, Scotland. Although it lacked people and counted in 1872 a mere 1,500 persons, mostly male, Winnipeg had other things in good supply: long, freezing winters with temperatures often minus forty degrees; mosquito swarms so virulent that horses died from their collective bites; and plagues of grasshoppers, which periodically descended on the adjoining farmlands with a Biblical vengeance. Winnipeg lacked sidewalks, pavements, waterworks, streetlights, and a sewage system. But it was not short of optimism. "Its newness was impressive," a recent arrival wrote, "its energy inspiring and its trade astounding. It might be called a city of bachelors, and these bachelors Canada's brightest sons; for if they do not possess intelligence and enterprise in a high degree, they would not be here. The retail trade of the entire province was conducted in Winnipeg, and the wholesale trade for a thousand miles beyond the western provincial limit. It was the capital and the country towns and villages all in one, and all the money expended by the Dominion Government on surveys, maintenance of volunteers, etc. almost immediately went into circulation in the remarkable city. For this reason, every inhabitant was wealthy — a few in reality, the balance in prospective. . . ."

Among Winnipeg's wealthy few, one stood out — a quaint, bewhiskered gentleman with erect posture and careful elocution who arrived one cool autumn day from the Old Country via New York City. Throughout the spring and early summer of 1873, Lord Gordon Gordon cut a fine figure among the ruts and puddles of Main Street and Portage Avenue. His Lordship was rusticating, it was said, taking in the good air, open spaces, and wild game of the frontier west. During a winter expedition at Brokenhead River, His Lordship "made a sensation and became quite a sportsman" by bagging 1,500 pheasants. Since elegantly outfitted "gentlemen's tigers" were scarce among the muskrats and

Winnipeg Manitoba, view from Main and William streets. His Lordship's "infantile and arcadian community" circa 1873. Manitoba Archives

buffalo, His Lordship took on as an assistant and bodyguard Mr. Thomas H. Pentland, who attended his hunting excursions and otherwise served as an aide-de-camp. Mrs. Abigail Corbett of Headingly, a small settlement ten miles from Winnipeg, provided Gordon with room and board and a barn to keep his horses in.

It was all very regular, sedate, above board. Vague rumors, it is true, about distant lawsuits, the Erie ring, secreted jewels, and contested bonds trailed His Lordship into town. But he did not elaborate much about the past or invent any new schemes. There were no changes of name or plans for grand, or petty, swindles. Winnipeg was a haven for him, not a prospective field of conquest. He paid his debts promptly, hunted, nursed his gout, attended cricket matches, and mingled with the local merchants and ministers, including Mr. John Schultz, Louis Riel's nemesis, and the Honourable James McKay, whose home he often visited at Silver Heights. Like the *Manitoba Free Press* and Métis discontent, Lord Gordon Gordon was fast becoming a local institution.

For the better enjoyment of his health and freedom, Winnipeg's isolation from eastern Canada was a godsend. After all, he had chosen this remote mud puddle, which posed as the gateway to the northwest, for one reason: to hide, amidst clouds of locusts and drifts of snow, from the mean swarms of Old World lawyers, detectives, bailiffs, and warrants. "Although essentially Canadian," a contemporary writer observed, "it was practically cut off from direct connection with Canada." Manitoba and its capital were recent Canadian acquisitions, dating back a few short years, to 1869, when Rupert's Land had been transferred to the new Dominion of Canada. The sole direct connection across Canadian soil was the costly and amphibious Dawson Route to Port Arthur, which was too difficult to permit the transport of supplies. Winnipeg's real links were to the south, extending across the border at Pembina towards the Dakotas and Minnesota. Telegraph communications to eastern Canada or the United States were routed through Saint Paul. Freight came by the Northern Pacific to Moorehead, 220 miles south on the Red River; then on to Winnipeg by steamer, flatboat, or freight team.

The commerce flowed north and south and with it came supplies, materials, and Lord Gordon Gordon's undoing. Just as Winnipegers visited Saint Paul and Minneapolis to trade flour and furs, lumber and hardware, so their American counterparts like George N. Merriam and Lawren Fletcher, Minneapolis lumber merchants, traveled north to buy and sell and wander over Brown's Bridge, which spanned the Assiniboine, or along the ruts of Main Street. It was during one of these excursions that the astonishing figure and person of His Lordship was spied among the baser folk of Manitoba.

Gordon's stay in Minneapolis had been brief enough, five or six months at the most; his impact on the region's political economy, scant. But Minneapolitans, from Captain J. J. Loomis to Mayor George Brackett, had never forgotten his lordly visitation, the poses and machinations, the Northern Pacific whirlwind tour. And they had followed, with incredulity, accounts of his subsequent career in New York, reproduced in local papers like the *Minneapolis Tribune* and *St. Paul Press*.

Although he had never himself dealt with Lord Gordon Gordon or been fleeced by him, Minneapolis Mayor George H. Brackett had more than a passing interest in the Gould-Gordon trial and Gordon's subsequent flight. It turned out that one of His Lordship's two original bondsmen, Mr. A. F. Roberts, who had assumed the burden of the entire $37,000 bail upon the untimely death of H. F. Clark, was a friend and business associate of the mayor. So when Brackett heard of Gordon's Winnipeg location, he wired Roberts, who faced forfeiture of the entire amount of bail posted unless Gordon could be returned to New York to face trial in time for the approaching autumn 1873 session of the Supreme Court.

Roberts wasted no time in acting on Brackett's intelligence. In mid-June of 1873, he consulted a firm of lawyers, pocketed a copy of the bail-piece, and traveled to Minneapolis where Brackett introduced him to a firm of lawyers and pair of policemen. Messrs. Lochren, McNair, and Gilfillan, all prominent Minnesota legal minds, apparently advised Roberts that, as bondsman, he or his designated agents had some sort of right, by common law, if not by statute, to seize His Lordship and return him bodily to New York "without legal process" — that is to say, without bothering too much about Manitoba courts, Manitoba warrants, Manitoba magistrates, national boundaries, or treaties of extradition, including the Webster-Ashburton Treaty of 1842.

To effect the forcible transfer, Roberts and Brackett engaged one Michael Hoy, a burly Minneapolis police chief and Civil War veteran — 10th Minnesota Regiment — and his associate, Mr. Owen Keegan, whose name was attached, at a later date, to one of Minnesota's ten thousand lakes. Hoy and Keegan were provided with several hundred dollars, a letter of credit for one thousand more dollars, guns, billies, handcuffs, train tickets as far as Moorehead, and letters of introduction to useful friends and collaborators in Winnipeg, including Mr. Merriam, Lawren Fletcher — the timber merchant and Minnesota assembly man who was subsequently elected to Congress — and L. R. Bentley, an ex-Minnesotan from Saint Anthony, who ran a store on Portage Avenue.

There were no hitches of any consequence. Hoy and Keegan left Minneapolis by train, switched to horse and buggy at Breckenridge, and arrived in Winnipeg on the afternoon of July 2. They went straight to Mr. Bentley's store, where Fletcher was waiting. A double-seated wagon was hired from the livery stable of a Mr. John R. Benson, who drove them to the vicinity of the Honourable James McKay's Buckhorn's Lodge. While his co-conspirators waited out of sight nearby, Mr. Bentley approached the house, engaged Gordon in a brief dialogue about Mr. McKay's unfortunate absence, and returned with the welcome news that His Lordship, prone on the front porch, was ready to be had. So they took him, after a scuffle and screams that roused the neighbors.

The run to Pembina was hectic. Gordon was held in the back seat between Hoy and Keegan, his legs and arms bound fast by halter straps. When he was offered a drink of whisky, which his abductors freely indulged in, he refused and asked instead to see a lawyer. They refused. While Bentley and Fletcher returned quietly to Winnipeg in Bentley's single buggy, Benson drove his own wagon over the toll bridge across the Assiniboine, without bothering to stop and pay the toll; found the Pembina trail; traveled all night; and, at around ten o'clock the next morning, approached the customs house several hundred yards distant.

The customs officials, Messrs. F. T. Bradley and F. J. Boswell, were ready and waiting, following the arrival of a pair of warning telegrams from friends of Gordon and from the attorney general of the province, who had learned of His Lordship's predicament from McKay's neighbors. As the Benson wagon, first sighted as a distant speck in Boswell's telescope, neared the customs house, Bradley ordered a halt and noted a pair of sheepish gentlemen in front, Benson and Keegan, and two more in back, Hoy and Gordon. When Bradley asked the worn figure in the back seat, shielded by Hoy, whether he was Gordon, the reply was "yes." And when Gordon explained further he had not come of his own free will but had been "arrested," Mr. Bradley did some arresting of his own. He seized the rifle from between Keegan's legs, ordered the abductors out of the wagon, and informed them that "there was no authority for an American officer to come into Canada and arrest a party in Canada; that there was a proper form to go through if they had any right to the prisoner." His Lordship, in the meanwhile, was freed from his halter straps, handed Keegan's rifle to better protect himself, and transported to Scratching River in Benson's buggy. From Scratching River, he returned triumphantly to Winnipeg, in the carriage of the learned attorney general of Manitoba, Mr. Henry J. Clarke, a vituperative Irish-born and Montreal-bred lawyer, who had done criminal law in Montreal and journalism in California during the gold rush, before finding his way to Winnipeg.

For His Lordship, the Pembina seizure was an Act of God, and for his kidnappers, the beginning of a long stay in the Old Stone Fort. Hoy and Keegan were returned to the Fort Garry jail, where they were joined soon after by George Merriam and Lawren Fletcher, who had been stopped at Scratching River by the attorney general himself, while attempting to escape south in a private conveyance. A day or so later, Mr. Bentley joined his friends.

The "Gordon kidnapping case" attracted wide attention on both sides of the border. "The best vindication of Mr. Gordon's cause," the *Manitoban* commented during the preliminary hearing, "is to be found in the fact that after he had crossed the schemes of the most powerful and unscrupulous Ring in the world, and after continued and acrimonious litigation on both sides, the only step they could think of to get his person into their power was one which involved a gross violation of British soil as well as a flagrant breach of the law and justice which should be common to all civilized nations." When Mayor Brackett of Minneapolis received a telegram from Fletcher, widely reported in the press as "I'm in a hell of a fix. Come at once," he rounded up a pair of lawyers including Mr. Eugene Wilson, later a congressional representative for Minnesota, hired a special train until Moorehead for $350, then took a wagon drawn by a pair of fast horses to Winnipeg, where he arrived in time for the preliminary hearing set for July 8, inquiring into charges the prisoners "did feloniously and without lawful authority, forcibly seize one Gordon Gordon of the parish of Headingly, in the said county, with intent to cause the said Gordon Gordon to be unlawfully sent or transported out of Canada against his will."

19

The Honourable Henry J. Clarke, Attorney General of Manitoba, Gordon's protector and tormentor. Manitoba Archives

The arguments at the hearing, between Americans and Canadians, Minnesotans and Manitobans, Minneapolitans and Winnipegers, dragged on for several weeks. The cause and source of the trouble, which erupted overnight into an international incident, testified for a full day about the awful circumstances of his seizure, then retired to watch the swords cross. The prisoners were defended by Mr. McKenzie, a partner in the attorney general's law firm, who took on the job for a substantial fee after Mr. Wilson, Minneapolis's leading attorney, was denied access to the court. The defense contended that Gordon was a fit object of removal by authorized agents of his bondsman, Roberts, who "under the common law of England, and wherever that is enforced . . . has a right to follow the party who has broken his bail, and seize and deliver him to the proper authorities without any other warrant than that of his bail bond." International boundaries, apparently, did not matter much. The sole intent of the accused was to restore the bondsman's principal to the proper authorities.

Judge L. Bétournay gave more credence to the arguments of the attorney general, assisted by lawyers from two local firms, who took time out in court to verbally lash the American consul, J. W. Taylor, for publishing in the local papers an open letter defending the actions of the accused. Deploring Mr. Taylor's missive as an "appeal to the passions of the mob" and contemptuous of the courts, Clarke informed the court of a telegram he had just sent off to the minister of justice urging the Ottawa authorities to press Washington to remove Taylor "from an office he has disgraced." With reference to the matter at hand, Clarke insisted that nothing less than a kidnapping had occurred; the intended forcible seizure and removal of Gordon to another jurisdiction in flagrant disregard of existing statutes, laws, or treaties. "There are treaties between friendly nations," Bétournay concluded, "to establish their mutual intercourse for their mutual protection on different matters, and chiefly against a certain class of offenders. When a crime of the class mentioned in such treaty has been committed in one country and the offender has escaped into another, legal proceedings are taken, and when the proper authority is satisfied of the legality of the demand for extradition, the party extradited has to be accompanied by an officer of the country through which he travels — no stranger could hold him." Judge Bétournay considered all of the accused implicated and ordered, on July 23, 1873, the five Americans — Hoy, Keegan, Fletcher, Bentley, and Merriam — to "stand committed to the common gaol of this Province until the criminal assizes for the province of Manitoba," scheduled for late autumn. An application for bail was immediately made, heard by Judge McKeagney, and refused to all except Mr. Merriam on the grounds that the offense was grave, the evidence of guilt strong, and "the power of [the bondsman] to take the principal was 'a personal right, confined to himself alone, and cannot be delegated to another.' "

The bail rejection went over badly south of the border. A mere pawn in a large dispute between nations, His Lordship faded momentarily into the background and was replaced as villain of the play by Attorney General Clarke, who was variously referred to in the Minnesota press as "a brutal blaguard," "the overbearing legal spider of Manitoba," and "the little Manitoba legal brute." Clarke, it was alleged, had orchestrated the entire affair and had stopped at nothing, including blackmail and extortion, to further his own pecuniary interests. In a front-page editorial on August 1, headed "Our People Should Make Ready," the *St. Paul Pioneer* wrote of a likely second Fenian invasion, "swift, silent and terrible" vengeance, and the need to wrap Manitoba "in flames"; while its sister paper, *The Press*, warned that "the People of Minnesota and of the United States will recollect the debt they owe to the courtesy of the Manitoba public and they can rest assured that the debt will be paid."

The politicians, in the meanwhile, traveled east in search of help, political and diplomatic. Governor Horace Austin, Senator Ramsey, and Mayor Brackett called in at the State Department and interviewed Mr. J. C. Bancroft Davis, the assistant secretary of state. The British ambassador to Washington, Sir Edward Thornton, was enjoined to help out. President Ulysses Grant was visited at Long Branch, New Jersey, as was Secretary of State Hamilton Fish at his summer home on the Hudson River. Roberts's New York lawyers retained legal help in Ottawa and Montreal. For weeks, telegrams flew back and forth between and among Minnesota's Governor Austin; Manitoba Lieutenant Governor Alexander Morris; the governor general of Canada; the prime minister and minister of justice of Canada, Sir John A. Macdonald; and the American president and his secretary of state.

The interventions brought results. In mid-September, almost two and one-half months after the prisoners' incarceration, Governor Austin arrived in Winnipeg to attend a special court hearing scheduled for September 15, 1873. It was all smiles, nods, handshakes, and neighborliness. By previous arrangement, all of the accused, with the exception of Congressman Fletcher, pleaded guilty and received nominal, twenty-four-hour sentences. The charges against Merriam were dropped. Fletcher's trial was postponed until winter and never proceeded with. On September 17, the entire contingent, prisoners and governor, left on the steamer *Dakotah* for Minneapolis, where they were greeted on arrival by three thousand cheering people, a pair of brass bands, and a contingent of Irish rifles. After a noisy procession and round of receptions culminating in a free-for-all at Brackett's Hotel, the great Gordon kidnapping case was laid to rest.

And what of His Lordship? Did he rest as well? Unfortunately, not. The Pembina rescue and subsequent trial invited an orgy of publicity and ended any prospects of a quiet retirement in arcadian Winnipeg. While the *Manitoban*, an organ of the Clarke government, saw fit to defend His Lordship on occasion as the persecuted victim of Yankee tycoons and champion of Her Majesty's stockholders against the great

Erie ring, its rival, the *Free Press*, indulged in brutal satire and disclosure on its front pages, where the whole range of Gordon's past activities and pretenses — from Yeovil to Wall Street — were given prominence. When Lord Gordon Gordon first sauntered down Main Street in October or November of 1872, only vague, ethereal rumors had floated about his regal head. Less than a year later, the full life story of "The Most Consummate Swindler of the Age" burst over Winnipeg like the dark clouds of a prairie rainstorm.

The publicity was bad enough. The harrassment and squabbles with Attorney General Clarke and his legal cronies made things a lot worse. His Lordship was reputed to be a wealthy man, as a result of his wheeling and dealing with the likes of the two Jay's, Cooke and Gould. It was thought, among Manitoba's greedy arcadians, that he owned plate, jewels, bonds, and cash, stashed here and there in luggage, dressers, mattresses, and trouser pockets. So the lawyers and the attorney general himself pressed for a cut. Throughout the summer and fall, Lord Gordon Gordon complained bitterly to friends like John Schultz and to Lieutenant Governor Alexander Morris, whom he petitioned several times, that Clarke had waved incriminating files past his nose, threatened hardships, begged him to hire his services to handle civil suits against the Americans, or to buy lots he owned downtown for ten or twenty thousand dollars. Mr. Frank Cornish, the former London mayor, Winnipeg's mayor-to-be, and charismatic rogue, who had assisted Clarke during the kidnap trial, also sought kindnesses and, according to Gordon, received as gifts an expensive diamond ring, a solid silver revolver, and $1,400 in cash.

So acrid did Winnipeg's air become during the heat of the kidnapping excitement that His Lordship planned a western vacation, or relocation, to a distant arcadian community over the Pacific mountains — British Columbia. After a noisy quarrel with Mr. Cornish at the Corbetts', over fees presumably, Gordon quietly left Winnipeg in early August, accompanied by horses, carts, provisions, and his faithful companion, T. H. (Harry) Pentland. The Second Gordon Expedition, a less extravagant venture than the Northern Pacific tour to Pelican Rapids, pushed slowly westward through Cree and Métis country, past Small Lake, Pine Creek, and Fort Ellis on the Assiniboine, towards the beautiful Qu'Appelle valley in Saskatchewan country. Métis freighters were hired and fired, and horses and carts exchanged with local nomads until, near the Touchwood Hills in the south Saskatchewan territory, the expedition counted six horses and five carts loaded with flour, pemmican, other provisions, and ammunition.

But here it ended. Alerted about His Lordship's departure on a hunting expedition "to fill up the time before the Fall Trial of the

Americans," the attorney general quickly dispatched in pursuit a party led by the chief constable of the province, Mr. Richard Powers, who had earned some sort of reputation for "single handedly subduing and arresting four drunken men." Being a mounted policeman or, more correctly, a policeman mounted, Powers's chase was epic and covered over several weeks 400 miles until it reached, in the dead of night, a telling willow bush in the Touchwood Hills. Although he had nearly famished from hunger and thirst along the way and had saved himself only by begging provisions from passing carts, Powers and a fellow constable had enough energy and ammunition left to invade His Lordship's camp in the early morning hours. "Gordon Gordon come out!" His Lordship discerned, among the chirps of morning sparrows and the buzz of mosquitos. So he exited from the willows, surrendered his weapons, and returned a wearying 400 miles with Powers, whom he later accused of drunkenness and the attempted robbery of $1,000 in cash.

The Honourable Henry J. Clarke, in the meanwhile, had arranged a special homecoming. "We arrived at Winnipeg on Sunday, September 14th," His Lordship wrote the lieutenant governor, "and on our arrival were at once taken to the police station and though I demanded to know could not ascertain what was the charge made against me. About 10 P.M. the Attorney General came into the police station and addressing me said 'Gordon you have outwitted the whole world but it shall never be said you outwitted me. I have you in my power and will send you to The Stone Fort for ten years.' Wherein I charged him in the presence of Mr. Pentland and other witnesses with his villainy in trying to extort money from me under threat — for this he ordered me to be locked up in a cell. . . ."

Having settled matters with the Americans, who received their nominal sentences the next day, Clarke turned his full attentions to Gordon and laid charges against him of perjury, forgery, and larceny — forgery and perjury, apparently, because he had signed and announced himself in court as Hubert Charles Gordon instead of Gordon Herbert Charles Gordon, and larceny because a Mr. Stalker of Headingly was ready to swear that His Lordship had lifted an awl from his livery stable. The Clarke-Gordon duel heated through the autumn and winter months of 1873. Gordon applied for bail and was freed on recognizance of his friends Messrs. Schultz and Brown. Postponements, stays, charges, and countercharges filled the air until the Clarke ministry mercifully fell during the spring legislative session of 1874. Weak and sickly, Gordon's tormentor departed in mid-July for a lengthy vacation in California. But he changed trains along the way in Saint Paul, Minnesota and was met at the station by Michael Hoy, who struck him on the head with a blunt instrument and kicked and beat him mercilessly until he almost died.

Clarke's removal did not end Gordon's troubles. Sickly himself, with heart trouble, he settled with his loyal Pentland at Abigail Corbett's Headingly home, took in her crops, played out his final role — as yeoman farmer — and awaited the inevitable. It arrived in late July from Toronto, where a trim gentleman, calling himself Mr. Hardy, checked in at Rossin House, a local hotel. Hardy's real name was Strachan, the New York lawyer who, for an entire two years, had ached for revenge.

Hardy's way had been prepared by Montreal and Toronto law firms who were friendly with a local Toronto police magistrate, A. MacNab. A meeting with MacNab produced some sort of warrant for Gordon's arrest, which was handed over for execution to a Toronto constable, Mr. A. Munroe, who took on the job with the blessing of Major Draper, the chief of police. Hardy and Munroe left the next day for the Great Western Railway Depot, where they were joined by a Mr. Ried, introduced to Munroe as "a friend" of Hardy's and likely an American detective. From here, the Gordon hit squad hopped a steamer to Duluth, Minnesota and arrived in Winnipeg on Friday, the thirty-first of July.

The final way to His Lordship's Headingly sanitorium was cleared by a local agent of the eastern lawyers, the Winnipeg attorney John Farquhar Bain, who first steered the invaders to the residence of Magistrate Gilbert McMicken. A "somewhat neurotic" recent arrival in Winnipeg, who had traveled part way from Ontario in a coffin, to keep safe the large sums of government money in his possession, McMicken signed and backed the Toronto "warrant" without bothering to read it and consented, verbally and in writing, to the direct removal of His Lordship to Toronto or, more likely, south to New York, without recourse to a local court or access to legal counsel.

The assault was now ready. After arming Munroe with return tickets, via the Dawson Route, which facilitated an easy border crossing into the United States at Rainy Lake and other points, Hardy and Ried withdrew to a local hotel since, as Munroe was informed, Gordon would doubtless recognize them on sight. Two local accessories, Messrs. George McMicken and a Mr. Fullerton, were then sent on a reconnaissance mission. They knocked at the Corbetts' front door, discovered His Lordship at home with Pentland and Mrs. Corbett, and engaged him in a brief discussion about the loan of a mare. Some wine was shared. Soon after their departure, the same gentlemen returned with Bain and Munroe, who presented His Lordship with the Toronto "warrant," informed him of their imminent departure, and clapped on a pair of handcuffs.

His Lordship caused no trouble. He merely asked Bain where they were going to take him. Bain replied that he had nothing to do with the matter. He then asked whether he could see his lawyer, Mr. Cornish, on

25

the way out of town. Munroe said that he could, for a few minutes. Gordon gave Pentland directions about the disposition of his goods and dressed for the road, following removal of the handcuffs. Missing his Scottish toque, he withdrew momentarily into his bedroom towards a table which held the cap and a pair of guns. He grabbed a gun, pointed it towards his head, turned towards the wall, protested that he would never be taken alive, and pulled the trigger. Munroe rushed over as Gordon collapsed in a sitting position between the wall and the bed. Blood oozed out of his left ear. He was dead in seconds.

His Lordship's suicide caused a real stir. Pentland held back tears at the coroner's inquest and told the court that, as far as he knew, his master had died a poor man, virtually propertyless. Mrs. Corbett offered the view, at the same inquiry, that Gordon was "a very brave man" who knew for a long time that the end was near. Chief Justice Wood complained of irregularities, chastised McMicken for backing an illegal warrant and Bain for collaborating in the sordid affair.[3] The *Manitoban* and several city councillors inveighed against Yankee invaders. And, in Edinburgh, Scotland, Mr. Thomas Smith, of the gentle firm of Marshall and Sons, goldsmiths, of Number 87, George Street, closed the delinquent account of a deceased lord.

---

3. The chief justice concluded that "no one could follow the evidence which had been given without coming to the conclusion that the design of the parties concerned in the arrest was to convey Gordon, not to Toronto, but to New York. The route selected, over Rainy Lake, and the arrangements made to carry him away the same night without opportunity of being examined before a Manitoba magistrate or obtaining legal advice, the conduct of the two Americans, and every fact, indeed, brought out in the evidence at the inquest pointed in the same direction." Had the party actually got off with Gordon, Judge Wood went on, "he would have considered it his duty to have had them followed and brought back under arrest." As to the "warrants," he described one as "simply illegal" and the other as "probably spurious" (*Manitoban*, August 8, 1874).

2
DEAD END

When the steamer the *Enterprise* jammed into a grassy bank at the mouth of the Homathco River, one foggy morning early in the month of April, 1863, it unloaded an unlikely cargo of provisions, mules, and men intent on building a wagon road to connect up the gold fields of upper Fraser River with the coast of the mainland colony of British Columbia. Amongst the disgorged party, which included ninety-one workmen, several tourists, a settler or two, and an artist taken with the prospect of painting glaciers, was the founder of the enterprise, Mr. Alfred Waddington, a gouty, sixtyish bachelor from Victoria, whose wish to build a road had become, in recent years, a positive obsession.

The source of Waddington's mania lay east of Vancouver Island, across the Strait of Georgia, in the new mainland town of New Westminster, which vied with his beloved Victoria for the spoils of the gold trade. Both places were offsprings of the gold rush, and both sought to monopolize the commerce flowing to and from the fields in the interior. A sleepy Hudson's Bay Company trading fort until 1859, peopled with staid Scotchmen and devoid of noise, bustle, gamblers, speculators, or "interested parties to preach up this or underrate that," Victoria was transformed overnight into a thriving business community by the flood of immigrants from San Francisco, following the spread southward of news that gold had been discovered on the banks of the Thompson River. But its pioneer gentry, of which Alfred Waddington was a prominent member, quaked at the prospect of losing their hold on the business to their mainland cousin, New Westminster, seat of a rival shopocracy and, since 1859, capital of the new mainland colony of British Columbia.

Amongst Victoria's budding civic leadership, there were few as dedicated to the high purpose of securing its eminence — and making a sizable profit in doing so — as Alfred Waddington. Son of an English businessman, Waddington joined the frontier trek north to Vancouver

Island following an uncertain business career in France and a more successful venture in San Francisco, as senior partner in the wholesale grocery firm of Dulip and Waddington. Waddington was delighted with his rustic new home and quickly entered into the business and public life of the colony of Vancouver Island. He established his dry-goods business, dabbled in property, served as treasurer of the Firemen's Charitable Fund, and, in 1860, entered the Legislature.

As businessman, publicist, and politician, Waddington devoted his modest literary and lobbying talents to the good causes of commercial growth and civic improvement. Though past his prime, he remained an optimist, a booster, a believer in the bright future of his adopted place — the Island — and in the future of the vast interior of the neighboring mainland colony of British Columbia, which faced it across the Strait of Georgia. He fought for the incorporation of Victoria; built an impressive

Mr. Alfred Waddington, founder of the Bute Inlet Wagon Road Company. Provincial Archives of British Columbia

cistern, at his own expense, on the corner of Johnson and Waddington streets; argued for a local mint; and, in a pamphlet written in 1859 (entitled "The Necessity of Reform"), called for constitutional changes to limit the power of the Hudson's Bay Company, which, to his mind, obstructed commercial development. "Now that a more enlightened population has taken possession of the country," he wrote, "the object of the company for the purpose of civilization is at an end, and its intervention for commercial purposes a nuisance." Waddington's head-strong optimism and lively advocacy of commercial expansion were nowhere better expressed than in his *The Fraser Mines Vindicated; Or, The History of Four Months*, the first book, aside from government publications, to be published on Vancouver Island. In it, he captured the spirit of the Fraser River gold craze, sketched its course in sympathetic detail, and proclaimed his faith in the future expansion of the new frontier. Here too could be found the seeds of his folly, the fatal vision that increasingly absorbed his energies soon after his entry into the Legislature in 1861.

Alfred Waddington dearly wished to link, by wagon road, the rich gold fields of the Cariboo with the coast of British Columbia at Bute Inlet — an arm of the Pacific Ocean penetrating the mainland's coastal range, approximately two hundred miles north of Victoria. Events following publication of his Fraser Mines vindication confirmed his optimism and spurred his purpose. The discovery of gold at Hill's Bar, outside Fort Yale, in 1858, was followed by a succession of other finds up to and beyond the month of the Quesnel River, whose diggings in the summer of 1860 gave employment to some six hundred miners. As hordes of miners poured up the canyon in search of the precious metal, new bars and creeks were brought into production in rapid succession at Ferguson's Bar, Keithley Creek, Antler and Goose Creek, and, in 1861, at Williams Creek, one of the richest gold fields in the world. "New discoveries followed one another in quick succession," historian A. G. Morice wrote, "until the Cariboo Mountains, which so far had known hardly any other sound than the hoot of an owl, the occasional stomp of the deer, and the shrill note of the Carrier's love-song were now alive with the thump of the miner's pick and the rattle of his rocker."

The echoes of picks and rockers were heard as far as New Westminster and Victoria where a host of promoters and politicians, Waddington among them, pondered ways of commanding the diverse benefits of the new trade. The miners needed routes and roads to bring men and equipment to the bars and creeks, ship out the gold, and transfer supplies and provisions. And promoters and politicians, eager for growth and profit, were prepared to aid the cause and "open up the country" by building roads. To this purpose, a pair of competing wagon roads were constructed with the aid and encouragement of Governor James Douglas: one by way of Port Douglas on the north shore of Harrison Lake, connecting up with Lillooet, and the other through Yale, by Boston Bar, Lytton, Alexandria, and up to Quesnel. The Cariboo Wagon Road, as it was called, was extended in 1865 to Barkerville, the heart of the diggings of the new gold empire.

However attractive to the New Westminster merchants, neither of these routes pleased Alfred Waddington, who felt they were too lengthy, expensive to build, and dependent on land travel as opposed to the more economical water transportation. More important, they threatened the hegemony of Victoria as a point of entry to ocean-going vessels, which might bypass the Island capital in favor of direct passage to the strategically-placed New Westminster. As an alternative, Waddington projected a route from Victoria by steamer to the head of Bute Inlet — where he and several prominent friends had preempted land — through the scarcely explored Cascade Mountains via the Homathco River, across the great Chilcotin plains to Puntzi Lake, and beyond to Alexandria and Quesnel, the heart of the new upper Fraser gold frontier.

Waddington's Bute Inlet scheme, as it came to be known, had certain apparent advantages, which its sponsor never ceased repeating following his resignation from the Legislature in 1861. At public and private meetings with legislators and merchants, investors and laborers, Waddington, aided by a packet of charts and figures, outlined the merit of his project. He argued that the distance from the Cariboo's gold core to Victoria would be shorter by almost a hundred miles in comparison with the Yale route; travel time reduced by fifteen days; the proportion of sea, lake, and river navigation, as compared to land travel, reversed. Finally, the development of Bute Inlet two hundred miles north of Victoria along Georgia Strait, would help to preserve the Island capital's hegemony as a point of entry for ocean-going vessels as well as open up for settlement the splendid Chilcotin plains, rich with bunch grass and suitable for agriculture and ranching.

Not all of Waddington's time was spent in Victoria cultivating politicians and drumming up investor support. Following a favorable report from surveyor Henry McNeill, who had explored the route from Fort Alexandria on the upper Fraser to the head of Bute Inlet, Waddington and a party of supporters departed up the coast in September, 1861, on board the steamer the *Henrietta*, then sailed a scenic thirty-two miles eastward, past mountains curtained with glaciers and peaked with snow, to the head of the inlet. From here, the party pressed inland along the Homathco River to a point within one and a half days travel of the Chilcotin plains. A second expedition, led by a Robert

Homfray, met with a succession of setbacks, including the loss of equipment, immobilizing snowfalls, gulf storms which kept six men in a single canoe for nine days before arrival at the head of Bute Inlet, and several run-ins with unfriendly Indians, who almost put the entire exploratory party to death.

The Homfray party's indifferent success failed to deter Waddington from pressing ahead with his campaign for support from government and private investors. A Bute Inlet Wagon Road Company was formed and the names of an impressive list of local dignitaries were added to the board of directors. Victoria's *Daily British Colonist* printed enthusiastic accounts of the scheme's prospects and progress. Modest sums of capital were raised at public meetings where potential subscribers heard of an agreement between the new firm and the colonial government providing for the construction of bridle paths and, later, a wagon road connecting Bute Inlet with the upper Fraser gold district. In return for a charter granting it the right to collect tolls for five years — later modified to ten — the company agreed to complete the road within a year. Several extensions were later granted, up to the end of 1864.

Soon after the signing of the agreement — on February 28, 1862 — an advance force of Waddington's men sailed to the inlet's head and commenced the punishing task of carving a path through the raw wilderness stretching northeast beyond the mouth of the roaring Homathco. While surveyors probed the way along the river's east branch as far as Fort Alexandria — and back along the west branch — a work force of seventy men pressed slowly onward, shaping the beginnings of a trail and constructing bridges across the numerous streams and gullies that cut into the river valley. Their work continued until late November, when supplies ran out.

The arrival of the *Enterprise* with its weighty cargo, in April, 1863, began the second full season of the Waddington brigade's assault on the Homathco. As the replenished work party quickly discovered, a formidable task awaited them. Their predecessors had advanced a bare few miles beyond the inlet's head, and many of their hastily constructed bridges had been washed away by spring freshets. But the men of '63 pressed onward, and it was not long before a primitive townsite took shape alongside the calm and beautiful sheet of water soon known as Waddington Harbour. Next to the site, across the river, stretched a luxuriant meadow abundant with pea vine and suitable for agriculture. A torrential nine hundred-foot waterfall nearby promised power for a sawmill and other industrial enterprises contemplated by the pioneer developers. A wharf was built, stables for mules put up, and lots surveyed. Several log houses were constructed by would-be settlers, together with a storehouse, which held supplies and served as the

31

temporary headquarters of the storekeeper and work foreman — a rough former employee of Waddington's in Victoria, William Brewster.

With the townsite as a base, the work party, aided by mules and augmented by Indians, edged eastward through dense woods of cedar and alder along the bank of the river which, widening at intervals, divided into shallow channels broken by stony islands. The surveyors led the way and were followed by the bridgers and choppers who, at a bend five miles from the river's mouth, constructed a second station from which supplies were forwarded to the camps ahead. The Slough of Despond, as it was known — thanks to several canoeing mishaps as well as the mysterious presence of dysentery nearby — hosted a storehouse, built on the high bank of the bend of the river, which afforded a splendid view of the land beyond. "The scenery from this point is much to be admired," Commissary Frederick John Saunders observed, "the bold and rugged outlines of the ever snow-capped mountains reaching from five to eight thousand feet high . . . contrasting magnificently with the dark green hue of the forest foliage of the valley, where the immense fir, pine, and even cottonseed abound, with a towering growth."

The Slough of Despond served as a major supply station until June when, at Boulder Creek, ten miles east, a log house was built in preparation for the crossing of the river. A primitive ferry was assembled and put into operation, consisting of a skiff and a scow attached to a rope stretched across to the river's far side, where a substantial storehouse was built, at Canyon Camp.

The expedition had now reached an awesome juncture: the foot of the great mountains that shielded the rich and rolling Chilcotin plain and lake country from the river valley and inlet to the west. At Canyon Camp, the roar of the torrential waters fighting through the gorge of the great canyon was clearly audible. "The scene here is awfully sublime," a C.P.R. surveyor later wrote, "the towering rocks, thousands of feet high — far above these again the snow-clad peaks connected by huge glaciers; and in a deep gorge beneath, a mountain torrent — whirling, boiling, roaring, over huge boulders always in motion groaning like troubled spirits, and ever and anon striking on the rocks, making a report like the booming of distant artillery."

The immense canyon and accompanying bluffs were more than scenic marvels; they were an invitation to despair, huge obstacles in the way of a quick and easy descent into the pastureland of the Chilcotin. Facing great walls of rock, steep gulches, and massive bluffs, progress slowed virtually to a halt. The blasting of galleries on the bluffs proved exhausting and painfully slow, while the departure of many of the Indian laborers for summer fishing at inland lakes depleted the labor force at the peak of the construction season. A self-appointed guide who materialized

The awesome Waddington Canyon on the Homathco River. Provincial Archives of British Columbia

33

from Bella Coola contributed to Waddington's chagrin by leading an exploratory party astray during an emaciating twenty-three days, before deserting altogether.

Stalled at the canyon, the Bute Inlet Wagon Road Company work-brigade was prepared, by late October, 1863, to call an end to the second full season of halting construction. As the snow line slowly descended the sides of the surrounding mountains, and autumn leaves, brown, golden, yellow, swirled lazily onto the valley floor, the several work parties withdrew to the townsite at the inlet's head where waiting large canoes carried them, in five-day voyages, to Victoria. To protect the stores during the approaching winter months and contemplate the great canyon's sullen resistance, several guards were posted at the townsite and inland camp.

The guards' protective concerns were hardly directed at the few white settlers at Bute Inlet, who were themselves troubled by the thieving tendencies of some of the Indians assisting on the building projects. To be sure, not all of the native laborers were perceived in a suspicious criminal light. The Homathcos, for example, a branch of the Coast Salish who congregated around Bute Inlet, were considered, as Commissary F. J. Saunders observed, "free-hearted" and "particularly friendly to the whites", a benign disposition they shared with a related tribe, the Klahuse, also deemed "friendly to the white people." But there were some Indians around who were perceived as bad; insolent and ungrateful wretches who, it was alleged, begged, stole, demanded goods that were not their due, and disappeared whenever their assistance was needed. It was to protect the stores from these Indians, some of whom arrived in spring and autumn from the land beyond the canyon, that the guards were posted at the townsite and inland.

The great canyon, as Waddington and his men knew, was more than a physical obstacle. It was a social barrier as well, separating the coastal tribes near Bute Inlet and at Bentinck Arm, the Homathcos, Klahuse, Euclataws, and Bella Coolas, from the roaming bands of the inland plains. A seminomadic hunting, fishing, and gathering people, numbering fewer than a thousand souls by the early 1860s, the Chilcotins — unlike their coastal cousins — had somehow insulated themselves from the culture shock produced by both the fur trade and, in more recent years, by the mining frontier. Sandwiched between the Carriers to the north, the coastal tribes to the west, and the Shuswap, Lillooet, and Fraser Indians to the east and south, the Chilcotins had never been Hudson's Bay Company favorites, and the trading fort established in their midst in 1829 was abandoned after more than a decade of unfriendly, and unprofitable, relationships. Nor did the church fare well among them. Missionaries, Catholic or protestant, had rarely visited their country and made little headway when they did. And when the brawling tribe of gold miners plunged headlong up the canyon, it was the neighboring tribes in and around the Fraser Canyon, the Shuswap and Fraser, who bore the first brunt of the invasion.

Although somewhat remote from the influence of the spreading white culture, the Chilcotins had evolved decent, traditional ways of making a living. Divided into bands and headed by local chiefs, they hunted, fished, and gathered roots and berries. Their territory covered several hundred square miles of rolling plains, grass, and hill country, and included several large lakes — Anahim, Tatla, Puntzi, Chilco, Benshee, and Chilcotin — where the different bands, two to three hundred souls at a time, congregated during the fishing season.[1] When they were not catching the fickle salmon with weirs along the Chilcotin River, they fished for whitefish, trout, and Kokanee at the inland lakes, trapped fur-bearing animals, fed off waterfowl, or pursued on horseback with bows and arrows — and later guns — the deer that fattened on the grasslands of the interior plains.

What the Chilcotins did not consume immediately or store for future use, they traded with neighboring tribes with whom they had established variable relationships of cooperation and conflict. The Homathcos, the Euclataws, and Klahuse to the west were all, at one time or another, enemies and the subjects of punishing raids, scalping, and mutilations. Similar wars were fought with the Shuswap and the Carriers. More benign contacts, however, developed with other bands and tribes, including the Canyon Shuswap and the Bella Coolas, with whom the Chilcotins sometimes wintered when the salmon runs failed.

When Mr. Waddington's light-skinned tribe of "King George Men" began their probes through Chilcotin territory in the early 1860s, they found many of the local residents ready and willing to engage in friendly relations of trade, commerce, and employment. The Chilcotins sniffed out the newcomers early, hired on as guides, packers, and laborers, and received for their services a variety of promises and goods including guns, powder, blankets, and ammunition. During his visit inland in 1861, Waddington engaged as guide a local chief, Tellot, who, in addition to more tangible benefits, earned an official certificate of accreditation. "It was his earnest desire to produce the paper confirming his importance," Commissary Saunders later observed, "and drawing from his breast a small package wrapped in many pieces of flannel, to the astonishment of all, it contained a piece of [the] illustrated *London News*, dated 1847, with

---

1. According to a Bentinck Arm packer, although the Chilcotins were often described as "horse Indians," they had "very few horses, only eight or nine being in their possession last winter" *(Daily British Colonist,* May 12, 1864). The same gentleman observed that the Chilcotins were well equipped with flint-locked muskets but short of flints.

the pictures of the ships "Erebus" and "Terror" starting from Gravesend, England, with Sir John Franklin's party for the Arctic regions. His character was written on its margin thus: Tellot, Chilcotin Chief, a good guide — faithful and trustworthy, etc. signed, Captain Price."

Tellot's kin were similarly utilized. Royal Engineer Lieutenant Henry Spencer Palmer's expedition from Bentinck Arm inland to Fort Alexandria in 1862, employed several Chilcotins as guides and packers, while Waddington's *Enterprise* was greeted, a year later, by a band of anxious supplicants, including several gaunt and needy Chilcotins, who squatted anxiously on the grounds of the future townsite. According to Waddington, the Indians awaited "their prey like vultures, and were not a little disappointed when they saw the mules landed and learned that these were to carry all the provisions." But mules, and white men, need assistance, and the Chilcotins, eager for guns and ammunition, were enlisted as packers and laborers until mid-summer, when they deserted for the inland fishing lakes. "There appeared a very marked difference in the Indians to those previously met with," the commissary observed before their departure for the Slough of Despond, which served as a labor exchange, "Their clothing was decidedly scant; their features were haggard, describing almost a hungry look. Some wore rings through their noses, and their faces [were] frightfully bedaubed with paint; the youngest men tying up the hair in a brush-like fashion at the side of the head, adding more to their peculiar appearance. They are of medium height, and speak much in the same twang as the Chinese. They seemed very anxious to trade for muskets and ammunition; bows and arrows being mostly used by them."[2]

Although squalid and worn in appearance, the Chilcotins who caught Commissary Saunders's eye were an energetic and broadly talented people. In addition to hunting, fishing, packing, laboring, and guiding, they were practical economists and possessed, as the Waddington work party soon discovered, a lively sense of their own land and labor's worth. From the outset, the Chilcotins' relationship with their white benefactors was strained and difficult. The whites expected a docile and grateful workforce, ready to accept pittances and promises in return for land and labor. Instead, the Indians proved stubborn and demanding, requiring,

---

2. Frederick Whymper later wrote of the Chilcotins: "These individuals had rings through their noses, are extensively painted, and are done up in the inevitable blanket. For the rest, there was nothing very characteristic in their costume, some having a shirt without breeches, some breeches without a shirt." The Reverend R. C. Lundin Brown, who came across a party of Chilcotins in the autumn of 1861, was not terribly impressed with their appearance: "a set of men and women more squalid and repulsive I have rarely beheld. Dark faces, with big mouths, high cheekbones, ferocious black eyes, narrow foreheads, long tangled hair, black as night; their thin and sinewy frames with little on them save dirt and a piece of blanket or a deer skin: no their appearance was not prepossessing."

according to Mr. Saunders, "no small degree of scheming tact in the management of them. . . ."

It did not take the Chilcotins long to realize that the white man's invasion of their territory was, at best, a mixed blessing that imposed on their lives and communities some terrible costs. Not the least of them was the dreaded disease of smallpox, introduced to Victoria in 1862 by a migrant San Francisco miner and quickly carried inland, into the Chilcotin country, by an exploratory party out of Bentinck Arm. The effect was devastating. "This disease spread so rapidly," wrote Lieutenant Henry Spencer Palmer, "that in a week, nearly all the healthy had scattered from the lodges, and gone to encamp by families in the woods, only, it is to be feared, to carry away the seeds of infection and death in the blankets and other articles they took with them. Numbers are dying each day; sick men and women were taken out into the woods and left with a blanket and two or three salmon to die by themselves and rot unburied; sick children were tied to trees, and naked, grey-haired medicine men, hideously painted, howled and gesticulated night and day in front of the lodges in mad efforts to stay the progress of the disease." When a correspondent for an Ottawa newspaper, who was traveling along Palmer's trail from Bella Coola to Alexandria, came upon the Chilcotin village of Nancootloon, he found it silent and deserted, except for the corpses, rotting in the sun, the faces turned upward towards the sky and shrunken eyes drawn into gaunt skulls. "When I saw flies crawling over these sightless and decaying bodies, I almost wretched," he recalled; "we . . . saw in many of the houses, corpses that had been deserted when their owners were still alive. We saw signs of a fight against the relentless enemy, a sudden conquering fear, and a flight by all those who could flee leaving their dead unburied, and their sick to become dead, uncared for." The dead's sole companions were infected blankets left by their relatives, which two white men from around Bella Coola, Mr. Angus McLeod and Jim Taylor, quietly possessed and resold for a handsome profit to unsuspecting Indians. The result was a vicious recurrence of the contagion.

The Chilcotins engaged by Mr. Waddington's crew were, in fact, survivors of a plague that had destroyed half their number and left the remnant in a semistarved state, dependent in part on the philanthropy of enterprises like the Bute Inlet Wagon Road Company. The company proved a mean and uncertain benefactor. By the spring of 1864, the entire project was in a sorry financial state. The construction slowdown; the competitive threat from a rival company, which received a charter to construct a road out of Bentinck Arm to Alexandria; campaigns of ridicule from the *Victoria Evening Express* and New Westminster's *British Columbian*, the refusal of the colonial government to subsidize the effort or even to provide protection for the construction crew created bitter problems for Mr. Waddington, who, short of working capital, was forced to sell off large portions of his personal property to sustain a scheme deserted by investors. Among the casualties were several white workers, including the foreman, Mr. William Brewster, who waited out the entire 1863 work season before receiving his wages. Others were allayed with scrip giving them a lien on the road company's charter.

But those who suffered most, at the bottom end of the totem pole, were the Indians, who quarreled with Brewster over the terms of alienation of their land and labor. "The Bute Inlet Trail had lately entered on their territory," a government report later summarized, "and no compensation had been offered them." When the artist Frederick Whymper arrived at Bute Inlet in the early spring of 1864, with a new work party, he found the waiting Chilcotins in a pitiful state. "The Chilcotin Indians are a dirty, lazy set," he declared, "and although a few Homathco Indians raised good potatoes at the head of the inlet, the former ... prefer half starving in the winter to exerting themselves. ... They disputed with their wretched Cayota dogs anything we threw out of the house in the shape of bones, bacon rinds, tea leaves and other such luxuries. Many of them are, however, willing and able to pack."

For their packing, the Indians collected pittances. In lieu of money, they were given promissory notes or accepted goods, mainly powder, balls, blankets, and clothing, from the company stores in quantities determined by Mr. Brewster. But they were unwilling to take food as wages, insisting on their right to be fed while employed. Brewster disagreed and, since the Indians claimed their durable goods, he refused to feed them. "When the whites would be eating," the Homathco Indian Cheddeki reported, "they would give a bit of bread to the children and the man in charge [Brewster] would take it away and throw it into the fire. They always made me and my wife eat in the hut so that we would not give any away."

Existing, and working, in a half-starved state, the Indians took to begging, stealing, and selling their bodies. The men pestered the white workmen with requests for food. According to one observer, "The women, particularly the younger ones, were better fed than the men as the price of prostitution to the hungry wretches was enough to eat." Stealing was common at the Bute Inlet townsite and at camps along the route.[3] At Canyon Camp, Commissary Saunders judged the Chilcotins to

---

3. Artist Whymper recalled the drastic remedy employed by a settler named Clarke to protect his possessions from a thief who crept down the chimney of his cabin. "Mr. Clarke lost last winter, many small things from his house at the townsite, and could not catch the culprits, who came down the chimney during his absence. At last he got a friend to go into the cabin with a quarter of a pound of gunpowder and locking the door outside himself,

be dirty, "thriftless," and thieving. "I was alone in camp at the time they came," he recalled, "and they certainly took advantage of the opportunity; for, while in conversation with Tellot, I could not be blind to the amount of thefts being barefacedly perpetrated, not only from through the chinks of the logs or house but from underneath the men's tents. . . ."

Following their return to Bute Inlet in March, 1864, members of the work party found that twenty-five sacks of flour, stored during the winter in a log house at the townsite, had disappeared. A search for the thieves led to bitter recriminations. When pressed by his white interrogators, an Indian replied, "You are in our country; you owe us bread." Enraged at the Chilcotins' surly refusal to admit their guilt or disclose the location of the flour, a white man carefully wrote down the names of the Indians present and threatened them with extinction. "I've taken down your names," he said, "because you would not tell me who stole the flour. All the Chilcoaten [sic] are going to die. We shall send sickness into the country which will kill them all."

Having barely survived several epidemics already, the Chilcotins did not take kindly to the threat. In the days following the resumption of the work inland, in April, 1864, a group of dissidents resolved to bring Waddington's entire enterprise, which had already passed several miles into their territory, to a swift and final conclusion. For an entire week, a powerful Upper Chilcotin named Klatsassin wandered in vain around Bute Inlet, anxiously inquiring after Mr. Waddington, whose arrival had been delayed by several weeks. Unable to locate the white chief, Klatsassin, accompanied by several young Indians, his two sons and daughter, and three women, set out on Tuesday morning, April 26, towards the ferry, on the first leg of an expedition to rid his land entirely of the white intruders.

Although a brave man and accomplished warrior, Klatsassin was likely aware of certain favorable circumstances attending his mission of extinction. Brewster's crew, strung out along the route, was unsuspecting and poorly armed, since most of their weapons had been traded away to the Indian workers. There existed, moreover, no reserve support, no white settlers to mobilize, or local military force on site and guard, preferred by a government cool to Waddington's scheme. A distant and tranquil backwater, Bute Inlet had hitherto been deserted by Her

---

went away a short distance and then crept back to watch the fun. Soon an Indian came stealthily along, his extremities bare, sans culottes, sans everything. He got nearly down the chimney when the man inside threw the powder on the smouldering ashes, and off it went. The Indian went off also, and with a terrific yell, but over the state of his nude portions I must draw a veil. He for months afterward, afforded a wholesome warning to his tribe, being unable to sit or lie down."

Majesty's warships, which were habitually employed off the Island and up the coast, to keep her unruly native subjects in awe.

Gunboats, constabularies, or posses were doubtless not at the fore of Klatsassin's mind when he arrived, on the morning of April 30, after sleeping over at the Slough of Despond and Boulder Creek, at the ferry crossing manned by Mr. Tim Smith, an ex-sapper of "violent character and irregular habits." Smith was despatched that evening with two bullets in his back, while sitting at his campfire. His body was dumped into the river nearby, the skiff hacked to pieces, the scow set adrift, and stores rifled of bacon, beans, coffee, tea, dried apples, and beef. What the Indians did not cache nearby or carry with them upstream, they scattered wildly around the site.

Klatsassin's war party departed the next morning for Brewster's main camp, located nine miles upstream at the foot of the difficult Third Bluff. Along the way, they met Chief Tellot and the Homathco Indian, Squinteye, who had been sent by foreman Brewster to pick up supplies at the ferry. Klatsassin advised them they need go no further, took Squinteye's rifle, warned him to stay silent lest he meet Smith's fate, and announced his intention to kill all of the white men, "because they did not give them their grub for packing." Tellot returned with the war party to the main camp, where they arrived before sunset on Thursday, April 29.

The evening was pleasant enough. The white work party, numbering twelve men, gorged themselves before retiring for the night to their several tents, where they slept in twos and threes. The Indians, numbering around eighteen men, as well as a contingent of women and children, danced, sang, ate, and plotted at their own encampment less than a hundred yards away. The attack came just before sunrise, with the entire white party still asleep except for the cook, Mr. Charles Butler, who had risen to light the morning fires. Butler was killed outside, with two bullets in the back; the rest were mercilessly assaulted, with a military precision, inside their tents. Armed with muskets, knives, and hatchets, Klatsassin's party divided into groups and attacked simultaneously. Few of their victims had a chance. The warriors whooped as they tore open the tent flaps and fired at their prone victims. Several ridgepoles were knocked down, the tents falling on the wounded or dead. Knives, hatchets, and the butt ends of rifles were brought into play to despatch the wounded.

Klatsassin's men performed efficiently, but they had so far missed the big prize, Brewster, who, with three workmen and an Indian cook, rose early that morning at a separate camp, a mile or two upstream, to begin the day's work of trailblazing. While Klatsassin and his colleagues divided the edible spoils and tore the lower camp apart, destroying books

Klatsassin's attack on Brewster's main camp as depicted in the People's Magazine *(1872). Provincial Archives of British Columbia*

and tools, a small party was despatched to finish Brewster's crew. They had no problem. The Homathco cook, George, was told to flee, which he promptly did, back towards the townsite, passing along the way the mutilated remains at the lower camp. Baptiste Demarest, a half-witted Métis, was so frightened that he ran for the water and drowned. The settler James Clarke was wounded in the leg, then disposed of with several shots and an ax blow across the head. A James Gaudet was riddled with bullets. Brewster received special treatment. Felled by a bullet and cracked in the head with an ax, his chest and stomach were cut open and the heart and intestines removed. According to a "friendly Indian," the heart was eaten. "The mutilation of Brewster's body was a well-known act of warlike vengeance," the *Daily Chronicle* reported, "and the natural consequences of being at the head of the enterprise in Mr. Waddington's absence."

Seventeen of Mr. Waddington's men were despatched in the morning raid. But there were three who miraculously escaped. "About daybreak," recalled Edwin Mosely, an Englishman who had joined the Bute Inlet project after a stint in the California and Cariboo gold fields, "I was awakened by two Indians coming to the door of the tent; they did not enter but raised it up and whooped; at the same time each of them fired on either side of me. I was lying in the centre. They then let the tent down; the ridgepole fell on top of me and the tent covered all three of us. While lying in this position, I saw knives on each side of me come through the tent, and pierce the bodies of my two companions. I could see through the side of the tent, and observing Indians going to the other tents, I jumped up and plunged into the river, which was about two steps from me."

The Homathco River saved Mr. Mosely, who swam downstream a hundred yards, crawled out onto the bank, then walked a further two miles before meeting the second survivor. The object of several misdirected knife thrusts and musket blows, Pete Peterson, a Dane, had likewise taken to the water, following receipt of a shot in the wrist. Faint with loss of blood, he followed Mosely to the ferry where, armed with a club, they barricaded themselves for the night in a cabin. The next morning, they were joined by the Irishman Philip Buckley, who had been abandoned for dead in a puddle of blood after a succession of knife wounds and musket clubbings had left him senseless. Buckley was a welcome arrival. A skilled seaman, he fashioned a loop from wire that, fixed to a guy rope stretched across the river, carried the three men, separately and slowly, to the abandoned ferry storehouse at the other side. Here they met two French-Canadian packers and a group of Bute Inlet Indians who, after hastily repairing the scow, accompanied the wounded men to Half-way House, fifteen miles above the Inlet's head. Large canoes, manned by friendly Indians, were used to complete the journey to the townsite and, several days later, to Nanaimo, where the survivors were warmly greeted by the local populace and provided with medical assistance. Five days later, in the early morning hours of May 12, the *Emily Harris* lumbered into Victoria's harbor bearing the Bute Inlet Wagon Road's sole survivors and their full morbid details of the Chilcotins' bloody deeds.

While the settler press screamed for revenge, and the Victoria and New Westminster authorities mustered forces of retribution, Klatsassin and his outlaw band advanced inland in pursuit of further white quarry. They found what they were looking for near Nimpo Lake, east of Bentinck Arm, where an expedition, launched by Waddington from Bella Coola, was resting after a 120-mile hike inland, towards Fort Alexandria. Led by the packer Alexander MacDonald, the party consisted of eight men, packers and gold diggers, their Indian auxiliaries, and forty-two pack animals laden with stores and supplies destined for the Cariboo gold fields and trail construction. MacDonald was not oblivious to the dangers ahead. Warned of Klatsassin's intentions by the Indian Anahim, chief of the western section of the tribe around Nancootloon — or by the Indian mistress of packer Peter McDougall — MacDonald ordered a retreat to a knoll several miles back on the Dean River, where a rifle pit twenty-five feet long, with flanking trenches on either side, was hastily constructed. Here, along the river bank, the men waited for two days without sighting a single enemy.

Tired of the self-imposed siege, MacDonald activated the pack train and ordered a withdrawal. They had traveled three miles, to a fork in the trail, when the waiting Indians struck. Stationed under the cover of trees and bushes on both sides of the trail, the Indians opened fire, stampeded the train, and instantly killed two of the packers, Clifford Higgins and Peter McDougall. MacDonald had his horse shot from under him and mounted another, which suffered a similar fate. Flat on his back, wounded, with a pistol in hand, he killed an attacker before succumbing to a pair of shots fired by Klatsassin and a second Indian, Yahoonklis, who was fighting at Klatsassin's side. The white men's corpses were left for the wolves to gnaw. Klatsassin's dead colleague was decently interred "in a siwash tomb of logs, pompously adorned with stakes and flags."

In the melee that followed the first volley, five of the white men escaped on foot and horseback and eventually made their way to Bentinck Arm. Along the way, a bloodied survivor, John Grant, burst into the house of John Hamilton, one of the few settlers along the trail, who had deserted his home at Canoe Crossing, twenty-two miles from the head of Bentinck Arm, only moments before the Chilcotins arrived. The Indians emptied his stores, just as they had earlier plundered the pack train inland of food and ammunition. The spoils were shared with the starved band of Anahim, the shrewd western district chief, whose men, waiting in the bushes nearby, stole from under Klatsassin's nose, and subsequently ate, several of the pack animals.

The decimation of the Homathco work party and MacDonald's pack train, together with the hasty flight of Mr. John Hamilton, had virtually cleared the Chilcotin country of white settlers. There remained, in fact, a single white encumbrance in the entire district: William Manning, a partner of Alex MacDonald's who had appropriated some Indian land, including a spring favored as an encampment by a local band, near Puntzi Lake, at the juncture of the Bentinck Arm and Bute Inlet trails.[4]

---

4. According to Judge Begbie, Manning's farm "appeared to have been formerly a constant camping place" of the local Indians, "but Manning had driven them off and taken possession of the spring."

Manning developed his property. He built a log house, cleared fields, and grew some crops. But the Indians resented his occupation. The instrument of Manning's deliverance was Tah-pit, an ally of Anahim, who attended while Tah-pit finished the job. Manning, it seems, was warned by his Indian mistress Nancy to flee, but he chose to stand his ground and died on it. Assaulted, unarmed, outside his house, and killed by a single shot, his body was mutilated, dragged to a spring nearby, and buried under a pile of roots. Anahim's colleagues subsequently robbed the house of food and stores, burnt it down, rooted out the crops, and, in a firm editorial on the sedentary life, destroyed the plow and other agricultural instruments.

Manning's death ended the brief and skimpy white settlement in the Chilcotin country. But it yielded the Indian rebels no real prospects of tranquil enjoyment of their plunder and patrimony. Like the Bute Inlet and Bentinck Arm massacres, Manning's death was merely an invitation to a larger invasion, by armed forces of white men, bent on revenging their kin's death, quelling a rising, and restoring order to a frontier rendered unsafe for settlement. "Wealth and industry are but unstable items in a country's prosperity if life and property become insecure," the *Daily British Colonist* editorialized on May 30, 1864, following the first news of what became known as the Waddington Massacre.

Now Waddington's enterprise had never been favored, in official or unofficial circles, as a choice instrument of development. Despite large efforts at lobbying, construction, and public relations, the Bute Inlet Road project remained, at best, a "scheme," the personal design of a restless bachelor unable to enlist the large support necessary to raise it to the level of a legitimate public project. "One of the most sanguine, imaginative men I have ever met," Chief Constable Chartres Brew commented on Waddington, "Prompt to delude himself on any matter of which he makes a hobby." Nor were the Indian policies, past and present, of the colonial government universally admired, in British Columbia or Vancouver Island, where critics spoke and wrote of an inept "bread and molasses diplomacy," "cunning and deceit," and "bad faith" in dealings with the various tribes. But critics and supporters of both the government and Waddington did agree on one matter: it was not — as a rabid editorialist noted — for "cowardly savages" to determine, through the application of force or otherwise, the fate of any white scheme, project, or policy; public or private, island or mainland. The news of the Homathco slayings and subsequent "outrages" caused great excitement among the pioneer citizenry of Vancouver Island and New Westminster, uniting friends and foes, islanders and mainlanders, in a great common cry for justice and revenge. "If treacherous savages can arise at any moment and interfere with the public or private works of the country," the *British Colonist* wrote, "there is an end to progression."

Of the many devotees of progress who were clamoring for smooth growth and a tranquilized interior, there were none who bore the weighty responsibilities of the new governor of the mainland colony of British Columbia, Frederick Seymour, barely a week at his job in New Westminster when the Homathco murders were announced. A slim, wan career administrator, summoned from the governorship of the British Honduras as a replacement for retired Governor James Douglas, Seymour was quick to arrive at an important distinction between good and bad Indians. The chiefs of the district of New Westminster, Fort Yale, Fort Douglas, and Lillooet, who, with their accompanying priests, met in New Westminster to celebrate Queen Victoria's birthday at the invitation of the governor, were, in Seymour's view, good Indians. Loyal and supplicatory, they expressed their wish in an address to "the great Chief English," to be friends with the white people and asked that their reservations, rarely visited by Seymour and subsequently reduced in size under his dominion, be "marked out for them." "Please give good things to make us become like the good white man," they pleaded, "in exchange for our land occupied by white men." Seymour responded with a free luncheon, "at great expense to the government," a free speech, in which he assured his guests "the Queen has a good heart for the good Indians," and "trifling presents." For next year's party, he had grander plans and placed an order with the Home Office for "100 small cheap canes with silver gilt tops of an inexpensive kind, also 100 small cheap English flags suitable for canoes 20 to 30 feet long." The canes, destined for use as staffs of office of compliant chiefs — as in the Honduras — were to be inscribed with crowns on their knobs.

For bad Indians, Governor Seymour had only harsh words and the promise of a just retribution, a sentiment shared by papers like the *British Colonist*, which urged the creation of a volunteer force to pursue the Chilcotin outlaws, "till every member of the rascally murderous tribe is suspended to the trees of their own forest." "I shall be . . . severe to the bad ones," the governor informed his guests at the Queen's birthday banquet. "I will punish them as they deserve." In furtherance of this objective, Seymour announced, through his secretary Arthur Birch, a $250 reward for "the apprehension and conviction of every Indian or other persons concerned as principle or accessory before the fact to the murder of any of the fourteen Europeans, who were cut up by Indians on or about the 29th and 30th day of April, now past, in the valley of the Homathco River, in Bute Inlet." Several days later, on May 15, he assembled and despatched to Bute Inlet a party of twenty-eight special constables, under Chief Constable Chartres Brew, in the H.M.S.

Governor Frederick Seymour who chased down the Chilcotin outlaws. Provincial Archives of British Columbia

Forward, a 104-foot gunboat armed with two howitzers and a thirty-two pound cannon.

Brew's was not a mission of annihilation. A sober and dedicated policeman, with a lengthy record of service in Ireland and the Crimea, he shared with his superiors no illusions about an easy capture. Brew's instructions were "to assert the supremacy of the law" and, it was hoped, induce friendly Indians "to capture and turn over the murderers." He found, however, that the Homathcos were deadly frightened of the insurgents and refused to advance as far as the death camp. As to the law's supremacy, Brew did enjoy modest success in affirming it, over a brief stretch of wilderness long deserted by the retreating Indians.

Chartres Brew's battalion, which counted Alfred Waddington among its members, spent several weeks tramping up and down Bute Inlet trail, piecing together the story of the massacre. At the ferry site, they found tools, bacon, and implements strewn about; several caches; a bullet lodged in a tree stump where Mr. Smith had been shot; but no trace of the body of the dead ferryman. At the main camp, the scene was horrendous. Broken pots and pans; bent cross-saws; shreds of paper, books, and bank notes were scattered amid blood-soaked sheets, pants, coats, straw-filled mattresses, and shreds of tents that had been torn up by the angry Chilcotins. There were no bodies, but ample evidence, through trails of blood and disturbed foliage, of where the corpses had been dragged to the river's edge before dumping. When Mr. Brew advanced toward the third camp, he found the going particularly tough and was able to reach his destination only after descending a steep precipice by rope and crossing a canyon on a single log. At the end of the trail, "which very much resembled the end of the world," he and his colleagues, aided by Mr. Waddington, located and buried under piles of logs and rocks, the bodies of Clarke, Gaudet, and Brewster, all badly decayed and mutilated. Donning his magistrate's hat, Brew held an inquest which concluded, "William Brewster, John Clarke and Jim Gaudet met their deaths by wilful murder committed by certain Chilcotin Indians, names unknown. . . ."

Facing supply problems and a treacherous ascent through the mountains requiring, at the very least, a large supply of horses, axes, saws, and ropes, Brew ordered a discreet retreat. Before departing on the *Forward* for New Westminster, which he reached on May 30, the chief constable composed a letter to the colonial secretary in which he alleged that the massacre "was far from being unprovoked . . . the Indians have, I believe, been most injudiciously treated . . . if a sound discretion had been exercised towards them, I believe this outrage would not have been perpetrated."

The colonial secretary and the governor, in any event, were not troubled about past discretions or indiscretions. Their sole aim was to capture the outlaws and, to this end, a second expedition was despatched west and southwest from Alexandria, into the wild terra incognita of the Chilcotin Indians. The chosen instrument, on this occasion, was a garrulous stipendary magistrate and gold commissioner from Richfield, Mr. William George Cox, who was directed to raise a force "not . . . sufficiently weak to invite attack, nor . . . so numerous as to form a heavy burden on the colonial treasury."

Cox's army was a ragtag affair. Miners and gold seekers "out of all nations" were joined by a smattering of gentlemen — officers emeriti of the army and navy who forsook, in favor of wilderness cookouts with Yankee roughnecks, "the refinements of the mess-room of the 200th or the highly intellectual conversation of the gun room of H.M.S. *Donnerwetter*." Bestowed with rude titles like, "Cap," "Mag," "Doc," and "Gem" and with commemorative names varying from "Doughnut"

to "Timber Jim," "Six Toed Pete," and "Wild Yankee," they floated out,
sixty-five in number, on makeshift rafts from Quesnel to Alexandria and
on June 8, began, in the company of thirty-seven horses, their long march
through woods, hills, and burned-out forests towards Benshee Lake, 112
miles distant.

Cox's army was no war party; nor was it intended to be. The
governor's instructions were to avoid military engagements or "colli-
sions," and Cox zealously pursued a strategy of avoidance. It took five
days to reach Benshee Lake along a route utterly forsaken by the fleeing
Indians, including the eastern district Chief Alexis, known to be friendly
to the whites around Alexandria, whose services were sought as an
intermediary. At Puntzi Lake, Mr. Cox discovered the body of William
Manning, which was decently buried, the memorial service being
conducted by Donald McLean, an ex-Hudson's Bay Company factor
with a long record of Indian warfare. Several search parties, armed with
Lancaster rifles, were then sent out, one of which beat a hasty retreat
following a brief skirmish with a band of Indians who dashed from tree
to tree whooping and firing as their opponents took to the bushes. For the
rest, Cox's army contented itself with destroying caches and fishing gear,
setting fire to the lodge houses of a village at Puntzi Lake, ravenously
consuming a month's supply of provisions, and constructing a rude log
fort on the summit of the hill from which a white flag of truce was
perpetually flown. A visitor to Puntzi Lake found Mr. Cox on the sixth of
July, almost a month after departing from Alexandria, "within the log
walls of his fortress . . . virtually besieged by an invisible enemy."

Governor Seymour, understandably, was not content to let matters
rest entirely in the prudent hands of Cox. Soon after the return of Brew's
party from its futile Bute Inlet probe, a New Westminster volunteer corps
was organized, headed by Brew, accompanied by the governor himself,
and consisting of thirty-eight men drawn from the disbanded Royal
Engineers. In response to a request from Seymour, who warned of "the
difficulties and enormous expense that an Indian War in this territory
would entail on the Imperial and local governments and the total ruin
which would befall British Columbia, were access to the gold mines of
the Cariboo rendered impractical,"[5] Admiral Kingcome at Esquimalt
volunteered the warship H.M.S. *Sutlej* to ferry the men to Bentinck Arm,
which had been designated as the launching point for a projected thrust
inland towards a rendezvous with Cox's army at Puntzi Lake.

The *Sutlej*'s arrival at Rascal Village, at the head of navigation on the

---

5. Seymour subsequently wrote: "It suited our purposes to treat officially these
successive acts of violence as isolated massacres, but there is no objection to our now
avowing that an Indian insurrection existed, extremely formidable from the inaccessible
nature of the country over which it raged."

Bella Coola River, was part of a grand naval exercise calculated to remind the local Bella Coolas of the Crown's continuing majesty and disabuse them of any notions of noncooperation. The Hudson's Bay Company steamer the *Beaver*, equipped with four brass cannons, together with the 202-foot-long warship the *Labouchere*, dropped anchor alongside the *Sutlej*, which, in commemoration of the accession of Queen Victoria, fired a royal twenty-one-gun salute. According to one apocryphal account, the roar of the guns "echoed back and forth from the towering mountain walls with such cumulative force that seagulls fell into the water from the vibration and had scarcely recovered when a further salute of 17 guns for Governor Seymour, shook the great trees of the forest as if they were willow wands." The governor, it seemed, had earned the title "God of the Mighty Thunder" among his rude subjects, who fled to the forest at the sound of the guns. "He is the mightiest thunderbird that ever shook our mountains," the Bella Coola Rosabella reportedly exclaimed. "I thought the sky was falling in."

The naval display and promise of rewards so touched the Bella Coolas that thirty of their number, under a local chief, volunteered to accompany the governor's party on the march inland. Progress was slow and uneventful until the nineteen pack horses, weighted with up to three hundred pounds each, stampeded during the long descent known as the Great Slide, from the valley of Bella Coola to the interior plateau. The result was "a bull-run on a small scale, pack saddles here, ropes there, flour, blankets, bacon, beans, buckets and a heterogeneous mass of fixens scattered along the trail in the most delectable confusion, all caused by starting before we were ready and stopping before we wanted to."

But the march resumed toward Nancootloon, Chief Anahim's stockaded village, which the volunteers found deserted. Several miles further, they came upon the scattered remains of the MacDonald pack-train ambush, which they first heard about near Rascal Village from several survivors who boarded the *Sutlej* for its return voyage. The trail and surrounding bushes were littered with kegs of nails, boxes of carpentry tools, gutted pack saddles, broken agricultural instruments, a shattered musket, yeast tins, ropes, candles, and sundries. The bodies of several dead men were found along the trail, their faces hideously contorted and bodies mangled by the wolves. The trail was strewn with the rotting corpses of horses that had been unable to escape the line of fire. Near the remains of MacDonald's corpse stood the rude log tomb, decorated with flags and stakes, of the single fallen Indian.

When the governor's party finally gained the shores of the Nimpo Lake, a few miles east of the earthwork barricade thrown up by MacDonald's party, it was noted that the Indians had fled, abandoning their village and crude fortress, loopholed for battle. The governor and

49

his men set fire to the fortress, inviting a single shot from a band of Indians, across the lake, who, at the first sight of the conflagration, abandoned their huts and migrated southwest, towards Bute Inlet. A "flying party" sent after them towards Lake Campana, headed by the governor's aide de camp, Lieutenant Cooper, and guided by a Chilcotin — who subsequently deserted — succeeded in losing the fugitives' tracks at the margin of the snows, after wandering for two days around the lake shore.

All of this preceded the arrival of the governor's party, on July 6, at Puntzi Lake, where Mr. Cox and his army were discovered barricaded and convalescent in their fort adorned with a white flag. The meeting was cordial enough, but the governor, perturbed by Cox's strategy of inertia, wasted little time in sending off the Cariboo magistrate and his men on a new search-and-destroy mission. Cox's army searched around Tatla Lake and searched again towards the head of the Homathco River, but nothing was destroyed except the life of Donald McLean, the old Fort Kamloops Hudson's Bay Company factor, who had come out of retirement from his farm on the Bonaparte River to join the expedition. A self-appointed avenger with a reported nineteen dead Indians to his credit, and charter member of the "New Caledonia Gang of Bullies" who, during a long and varied fur-trade career, had earned the hatred of many of the Chilcotins and their kindred tribes, McLean was ambushed during a foray in the company of a young Indian guide, north of the Chilco River.

McLean's demise had a chilling effect on Mr. Cox, who, with his frustrated posse, returned on July 20 to his makeshift fort at Puntzi Lake to report to the governor on the most recent lack of developments. The judge was greeted by a restive and hungry governor. Food supplies were running low, and a pack train despatched to Bella Coola for supplies was still in the bush. Had it not been for the few remaining Bella Coolas — twenty had deserted — and a party of Chilcotin women who established a "fishing station" several miles from the camp, trading trout for sugar, the governor and his men might have reached an embarrassing state of starvation. To make matters worse, several of the "majors" and "cap'ns" of Cox's army were getting itchy for action and contemplated waging a vigilante campaign against any Indians they could sight.

The governor, however, was spared this embarrassment by a welcome arrival — the Bella Coola pack train, which provided food, and good humor, for the restive troops and inducements for a long-sought-after guest, the eastern notable Chief Alexis. It was on a warm sunny day in late July that Alexis rode into camp, dressed in a French uniform "such as one sees in the pictures of Montcalm," followed by an impressive retinue, and seeking a personal interview with the Great Chief.

Alexis was an important personage among the Chilcotins, and his willingness to do business with the governor and enlist as an intermediary was an important development. Although Seymour "officially" treated the outlaws' successive acts of violence not as "isolated massacres" but as "an Indian insurrection ... [made] extremely formidable from the inaccessible nature of the country over which it raged," experience in the field had taught him, from the day of his removal from the *Sutlej*, that the rebels lacked both a way of rousing their brethren to war and the will to engage in a protracted military conflict. During two months of operations out of Bute Inlet, Bentinck Arm, and Alexandria, relatively few shots had been fired or casualties inflicted by the fugitives, who, in the familiar terrain of their homeland, had chosen to run and hide, rather than to stand and fight.

Up to the moment of Alexis's historic visit, Klatsassin and his allies had won some short-run objectives. They had plundered the white men's food and ammunition, halted the menacing trail construction, virtually ended the brief and sparse settlement, and, most recently, had confounded and stood off invading forces of armed troops. But any sustained rising they may have contemplated was forestalled not merely by a thin resource base and small numbers, but by divisions within their own and neighboring tribal groups. When Chartres Brew arrived at Bute Inlet, he was pleased to learn that the Homathcos, Euclataws, and Klahuse were fearful of the Chilcotins and loathe to join them, a reticence shared by the Bella Coolas at Bentinck Arm, who enlisted as auxiliaries to the white military expedition. Since moving inland, nothing further had happened to alter the impression of Mr. Brew or the governor that the outlaws lacked committed allies among their own and neighboring tribes. During his slow passage up the Great Slide, Seymour could boast of the "wavering allegiance" and docility of the local tribes, while around Nancootloon, where Chief Anahim held sway, there was no indication of any inclination to stand, fight, or join Klatsassin. As for the eastern notable, Alexis, he seemed more interested in collecting "inducements" from the newly arrived pack train than throwing in his lot with Klatsassin and Tellot's bands whom he described as *"des mauvais sauvages qui [ne] connaissent pas le bon Dieu."* According to the governor's aide de camp, Lieutenant Cooper, Alexis "professed to consider the whole affair as a war between the whites on the one side and Tellot and his men on the other, in which it was his duty to remain neutral."

Alexis, it turned out, was something less than neutral. So confident was Seymour of the loyalty of his new friend that he left matters in the hands of his two field commanders, and, on July 25, vacated Puntzi Lake for Richfield in the Cariboo gold fields, where the local roughs

51

entertained him at a reception so heated that "an honest miner simply pushed his elbow through the window, as the most expeditious means of ventilation." Alexis, in the meanwhile, lent his good offices to Cox in the delicate task of flushing out the rebels, who, short of food and provisions and fearful for the lives of their women and children, were prepared to negotiate a settlement.

The big break came in early August when the son of Tah-pit, accompanied by Alexis, appeared at Mr. Cox's camp on the Chilco River, bearing a message that the Indians were ready to meet and settle differences. If the whites persisted with their chase into the mountains, Klatsassin warned, they would all be killed. Cox countered with a promise not to harm the Indians if they agreed to join his camp on the site of the old Hudson's Bay Company fort on the Chilcotin River, just above its junction with the Chilco, preparatory to a meeting with the Great Chief. Klatsassin replied with a gift of twenty dollars in gold coin, as an expression of good faith, and a promise to appear four days hence at the appointed place with as many of his colleagues as could be fetched from the mountains by runners. As proof of his own friendly intent, Cox sent off a gift of several pieces of tobacco.

The Indians proved true to their word and at 8:30, on the morning of August 15, 1864, arrived, eight in number, at the camp of Mr. Cox. In the place of arms, they brought an assortment of gifts, including one and one-half ounces of gold dust, $5.50 in silver, $20 for the governor "as a token of good faith," one horse, one mule, and a mess of tobacco, which was consumed by members of both parties in an atmosphere so cordial that the Indians thought themselves perfectly safe. What followed, therefore, came as a terrible shock. On the orders of Cox, the Indians were quickly surrounded, informed of their arrest, shackled and manacled, and herded into a specially prepared stockade.

Klatsassin, it appeared, had suffered from a grave misapprehension based on assurances advanced by Cox and conveyed by Alexis, who had served as mediator and translator during the negotiations. "I promised them that I would not hurt them," Cox later protested, "that I had not the power to kill them — that I would hand them over to the Big Chief." Klatsassin, unfortunately, attached an entirely different meaning to Cox's messages — whatever their true wording and transmission secondhand — and took them to mean that he and his colleagues would be free to come, go, or camp wherever they chose (preferably with Alexis nearby), pending their meeting with the Big Chief, whose identity the Indians also seemed to have confused. Klatsassin thought the Big Chief was Governor Seymour with whom he intended to settle outstanding differences. Mr. Cox had another gentleman in mind — the justice of the Court of British Columbia, whose job it was to try, in a court of law, criminals, murderers, and like offenders. According to Judge Begbie himself, Klatsassin was "completely in the dark as to consequences of his entering Wm. Cox's camp on the 15th August" and "had been induced to surrender."[6]

Whether Klatsassin had been induced, seduced, enticed, or merely encouraged was no prime concern of Cox who, after two months of roughing it in the bushes, was prepared to lead his army homeward again, towards the Cariboo. Neither of Governor Seymour's commanders, at the moment of their departure, could claim to have captured all of the wanted criminals, but both were satisfied that enough of the core culprits had been detained to make a decent show of it. By Klatsassin's own admission, there were ten members of his own group, implicated in the Bute Inlet and related massacres, still at bay in the mountains and unreachable until spring, at the earliest, when they were due to come down to fish in the lakes. As to the evanescent Anahim and his followers, who owned most of the spoils of MacDonald's pack train, Mr. Brew took it upon himself to resolve matters in a gentlemanly way. During a final exhausting sweep through Anahim's country, Brew took up the wandering gentleman's offer to surrender, met with him, donated several gifts, and received a few in return, including several emaciated horses from the pack train, not yet eaten by the starving band. Brew also bought Anahim's claim that he had nothing to do with any of the killings and was ready at the first opportunity to deliver up some of the remaining Indians. "I know it was alleged that Anahim got a large share of the profit of which Alick MacDonald and his party were robbed," Brew reported, "I cannot say that such is not the case. . . . I am satisfied that Anahim knew nothing of the plunder and murder of Mr. Waddington's men til several days afterwards and all the Indians I have examined agree in saying that if Anahim had been at home Alick MacDonald would not have been attacked."[7]

Anahim was free, but Klatsassin and his colleagues had no other

---

6. Begbie later wrote, following an interview with Klatsassin, whom he described as "the finest savage" he had ever met with: "In answer to my question, whether he would have come in if he had known that he was henceforth to be in confinement up to his trial before me, and to be dealt with then for the murder of these men, he gave a decided negative." Begbie also acknowledged that Klatsassin had been confused about the identity of the "Big Chief" and had suspected Alexis of deception during the negotiations: "Klatsassin I think suspects Alexis—(a rival chief, who had everything to gain, both by receiving an immediate reward, renewing tranquility, and removing a competitor for influence)—of duplicity while he acted as interpreter."

7. Tah-Pit, at his trial, insisted that Anahim had encouraged him to kill Manning and, indeed, was with him when the murder took place. The chief constable's decision to exonerate Anahim was supported by the governor and Executive Council, and Anahim was eventually pardoned.

Sir Matthew Baillie Begbie who sentenced Klatsassin and four of his colleagues to death by hanging. Provincial Archives of British Columbia

prospects than the gallows, specially erected for them from local wood, at Quesnel, a frontier community set on the bare plains at the head of navigation on the upper Fraser River. While Chartres Brew wandered west and, after 107 days in the field, eventually left Bella Coola for New Westminster, Cox hustled his men and prisoners east to Alexandria where a steamer carried them to a makeshift prison, an improvised affair, "a mere log house, with part partitioned off for a cell." Here they remained — shackled, squatting, and brooding — for over three weeks, awaiting Judge Begbie, who arrived on September 27, the day before the commencement of the trial.

Begbie's stay at Quesnel — one of several stops on a trial circuit that took the Cambridge graduate through hundreds of miles of wilderness — was short. Translations were handled by a Métis, Baptiste, and a Mr. Fitzgerald, both of whom had a smattering of the Indian dialect. Mr. John G. Barnston, a lawyer and speculator with an interest in the Bentinck Arm scheme, served as defense counsel. The trial lasted for two days and resulted in the sentencing of Klatsassin and four of his colleagues to death by hanging. Charges against two of the prisoners were dropped, while a third, Cheddeki, escaped en route to New Westminster, after no witnesses to identify him could be found in Quesnel.

Klatsassin and his condemned colleagues were not spared a lengthy period of anguished waiting. Although it was accepted public policy to have executions immediately follow convictions, in line with Begbie's observation that "the difficulty of keeping safely men who know they are to be hanged is much greater than when they think they may get off,"[8] the hanging was delayed for almost a month, while the Executive Council, concerned about the circumstances of capitulation, considered reports from Cox, Begbie, and Brew. The condemned men, in the meanwhile, were entertained by a special emissary, an itinerant frontier missionary who occupied a vicarship in Salop after "promiscuously preaching to gold diggers" in frontier camps.

The Reverend R. C. Lundin Brown arrived at Quesnel on October 2, the very morning of Begbie's departure on the *Enterprise* and, upon hearing of the prisoners' sad state, resolved to console and bring them to Christ. When the Reverend first arrived at the jail, he found the prisoners heavily shackled, squatting on the dirt floor, "as wretched as could be." But they bore up manfully, he observed, because "they fancied themselves martyrs for their country."

Aided by the Métis Baptiste, who served as translator, Brown set to work on his captive flock, reminding them in Chinook and French of sin, wrath consequent upon sin, repentance towards God, and faith in Jesus Christ. And he spoke lovingly of a future idyllic state of peace and righteousness when the Indians would join with the whites and learn to pray, till the soil, engage in useful trades, and foster their own race of virtuous priests.

It was not easy going. Whenever the Reverend reminded them of the law against murder and consequences of Divine displeasure, the Indians insisted that they had "meant war, not murder," and had killed only in

---

8. Begbie later wrote to the governor, "it seems horrible to hang five men at once, especially under the circumstances of capitulation. Yet the blood of twenty-one whites calls for retribution. These fellows are cruel, murdering pirates—taking life and making slaves in the same spirit in which you or I would go out after partridges or rabbit shooting."

self-defense, as the whites had threatened them with a visitation of smallpox. Eventually, however, the Reverend reported that all came round except for Chessus, a bad Indian to the very end, who "when asked if he was sorry for his infernal treatment of poor Brewster's remains ... laughed like a fiend and said he didn't care." Tah-pit and Pierre, a boy of eighteen years, both of whom had been baptised, "seemed quite penitent," while Klatsassin and Tellot agreed, after a lengthy interview, to baptism. "They professed such earnestness in their desire to be baptised, and in the assurances of their penitence and faith," Brown recorded, "that I accordingly came next morning and baptised Klatsassin and Tellot, giving the former my own name and calling the latter after Baptiste. Their demeanor was most grave and convinced me still more of the sincerity of their repentance."

Klatsassin's enlistment as a "King George Catholic" as opposed to "Frenchman Catholic" could not have come sooner.[9] On October 24, the death warrant arrived from New Westminster and final arrangements were made for the hanging, two days later. On the frosty morning of their doom, the Indians prayed, breakfasted, and took holy communion before heeding, one by one, the call of the jailer for pinioning. Over two hundred of their countrymen, Indian and white, silent and respectful, attended as brief prayers were recited in the Chilcotin language and the ropes were adjusted around the necks of the blindfolded men, who trembled on the drops. Before departure, each heard, from the lips of the Reverend R. C. Brown, the words "Jesus Christ be with thy spirit."[10]

The Christian burial of the Chilcotin outlaws, according to Anglican rites, in a patch of woods outside Quesnel along the Cariboo Toll Road, was followed by a sustained round of backslapping, cheering, and petitioning in the colonies to the south. Editors rejoiced that the haughty Indians had been taught a lesson by a wise regime, which, forsaking a Yankee policy of annihilation, had exercised a laudable restraint in bringing the guilty parties to justice. The secretary of the colonies praised the novice governor for efficient work and was pleased to hear of

---

9. As the adopted son of the Reverend Mr. Brown, it was proper that he should describe himself in this way. Brown recorded in his diary that the prisoners, who had been exposed to several French Catholic missionaries, at first suspected him as being "not a right priest," since he said very little about the Blessed Virgin, who was at the center of Catholic teaching.

10. Prosecutions in the Chilcotin War ended in July, 1865, when Ahan, implicated in the MacDonald pack-train ambush, was executed after a trial in New Westminster. At the instigation of Anahim, Ahan voluntarily surrendered near Bella Coola and hoped to barter his freedom with a load of choice furs. Instead he was removed to New Westminster and tried at a special assize before the Honourable H.P. Crease who, according to a biographer of Begbie, "could hardly be said to be impartial," since he served in another capacity as the attorney general, the principal law officer of the Crown.

Seymour's own appreciation of the services of his men "engaged in a conflict formidable from the nature and extent of the country over which it raged and one in which it appeared at one time, as if famine were to fight on either side." "That Europeans should thus run down wild Indians," the governor exulted, "and drive them to suicide or surrender in their own hunting grounds in the fruit and fish season, appears to me, I confess, little short of marvelous."

But there were disappointments, and petitions, as well. Donald McLean's bereaved widow petitioned the Executive Council and was awarded £100 a year for five years. The colony petitioned the Imperial government for a subsidy to cover the cost of the war and was rebuffed by the colonial secretary, who noted that the war operation had been undertaken "exclusively in the interest of the Colony, and that the expense is in a great measure due to the high rate of profit which the colonists are realizing and therefore can hardly be viewed as any matter of complaint."

But the weariest petitioner of all was a portly Victoria gentleman, Alfred Waddington, whose undertaking, clung to like a fond and doting parent, had "led to such lamentable results." No sooner had the nooses tightened around the Indians' necks than Waddington was at the governor's door petitioning for reimbursement of the more than fifty thousand dollars he had expended, on the grounds, in part, that his party had not been afforded protection. He was refused, the governor replying that no protection had been requested and, in any event, "no state could guarantee its citizens against murder."

Although the wagon road died, Alfred Waddington's vision endured and expanded to embrace the concept of a trade route linking Britain and the Far East through a great overland communication system spanning British North America. He wrote several pamphlets outlining his ideas, lectured and lobbied in Ottawa and London, and, in his final years, was intrigued by the prospect of a transcontinental railway with its western terminus at Bute Inlet, of course. In the year of his death, from smallpox in Ottawa, in the spring of 1872, a C.P.R. survey party explored the inlet, which they eventually rejected in favor of the Fraser River route.[11] The surveyors experienced no Indian trouble, however, and found the local Chilcotins, or what was left of them, to be "the manliest and most intelligent Siwashes in the province."[12]

---

11. Waddington felt the railway should go via the Yellowhead Pass to Bute Inlet. He believed that the Fraser Canyon was too formidable and the river's mouth too shallow and marked by shifting sandbanks. The Fraser route's proximity to the United States of America was a liability as well, since the canyon could easily be blockaded.

12. The Crown colonies of Vancouver Island and British Columbia eventually joined in 1866 to form the United Colony of British Columbia which, in 1871, entered the Dominion of Canada as the Province of British Columbia.

3
THE SAGA OF RED RYAN

On a gray November morning in the year 1912, Mr. John E. Bell, a market gardener from Cooksville, Ontario, dozed comfortably as his horse-drawn wagon clattered along a small icy road west of Islington. Although Mr. Bell had begun the daily chores early, his progress was impeded, at around five in the morning, by a young motorcyclist whose vehicle violently collided with his wagon in a vain attempt to pass. Mr. Bell was understandably upset at the event, and when the cyclist, in the company of a pair of friends who had arrived on a second cycle, asked permission to load their wrecked machine onto his wagon for transport into town, he adamantly refused. This so angered one of the youths that he drew a gun, fired several shots over the gardener's head, and, whether by accident or design, glanced two bullets into the horse's haunch and flank.

The author of this shooting, which caused Mr. Bell to escape home for repairs and to call the police, was a slim, red-haired youth known to his friends and enemies as Norman John (Red) Ryan. Young Ryan's brush with the market gardener and his unfortunate horse was not his first escapade; nor was it fated to be his last. Both of the motorcycles involved in the incident, together with an assortment of goods and money, had recently been stolen by the Ryan gang, who continued their depredations soon after returning to their Toronto home base.

Their next target was Mr. John B. Hayes, a Queen Street West cigar merchant, whose shop was broken into in the early hours of November 26, and several pipes, cigarettes, and other small articles removed. In the course of leaving, however, the burglars dropped a cigar box, the clatter of which alerted a local constable making his nightly rounds. The constable entered the store, noted the open back door, and slipped into the dark backyard where the meow of a siamese cat signaled the flight of the culprits down a nearby alley. Two warning shots and a four-block chase resulted in the arrest of one of the burglars — Red Ryan — who, on December 3, 1912, was brought before Magistrate George T. Denison in the Toronto police court and charged with burglary, shoplifting, and theft.

The youth who stood before Magistrate Denison had red hair; small, alert, blue eyes; a charming manner; and a record of infractions dating back several years. Born in a small house on Markham Street in Toronto in July, 1895, Red was the fourth of seven children born to Irish-American parents. His father, a sheet-metal worker, sent him to Saint Mary's, Saint Francis, and Saint Peter's schools and encouraged him to enter the family trade.

Red had a pretty clean record until the age of twelve. "I was the same as other boys as far as having a merry battle," he later recalled. "Duck on the rock, hopscotch and nibs formed my early play days, just the same as that of all my boyfriends. I was nicknamed 'Red' and 'chicken' and took part in all of the games. I used to like to play with the girls, as well as the boys and was often called 'sissy' for this. I had great success in all of the games I played and there were none around our corner who could beat me in a 100 yard race."

Red, it appears, was also adept at throwing balls and, one day at an exhibition, lobbed four baseballs on target into a frame of little square holes. For this feat, he was allowed to choose a prize from among alarm clocks, jackknives, revolvers, and other articles. He picked a .22-caliber revolver.

With his weapon in hand, Red won new respect from his peers. "Naturally I was the envy of all my boyfriends," he later recounted, "and was looked upon thereafter as their leader." He hunted the neighborhood's stray cats, who fed in the garbage dump nearby, and one day brought a trophy home to his father, who thrashed him, took the gun away, and hid it in a bureau drawer. But Red knew its location and used the revolver at will. One spring day, he and a friend climbed a neighbor's cherry tree and filled their pockets. An old lady appeared out of the back door and ordered them down, after ignoring the boys' warning to get back inside the the house. "I fired a shot in the air," Red recounted, "and the rapidity with which the door was shut made me swell with pride. I believe that this was the first actual feeling that I had of the power of a weapon."

Red's altercation with the old lady had less serious consequences than his collision with the courts. On October 18, 1907, at the bare age of twelve, he appeared before Magistrate Denison on charges of stealing a bicycle and three dollars in cash. A year later, he was caught trying to steal some chickens and was sent to Saint John's Reform School, where a record of good behavior won him an early reprieve. But he returned to his old ways and on June 23, 1911, made a court appearance on theft charges involving, among other things, a gum box. Taking into account the minor nature of the thefts and Ryan's recent clean record, Police Magistrate Kingsford dealt him a light sentence.

No similar clement thoughts pervaded the mind of Magistrate Denison, on that frosty December day in 1912, as he stared down at the expressionless face of the youth he had not seen for five years. The charges against Ryan were more serious than any laid before, and his intermittent court appearances pointed to the making of an habitual criminal. The magistrate decided to take the matter in hand and grant society a lengthy reprieve by sentencing Ryan to three years on each of three charges, to be served concurrently in the Kingston Penitentiary. Ten days later, after hearing evidence about the Cooksville shooting, Judge Morgan added three-and-a-half more years.

Red Ryan's days of adolescent bravado had ended, and a new and crueler life began behind the gray stone walls of an edifice built on the theory that the inmate was "a creature apart, differing from other human beings, not amenable to the same influences, hardened by kindness, discouraged and made restful by cruelty." Kingston Penitentiary, at the time of Red Ryan's entry into it, did not discriminate between hardened criminals and young offenders, murderers and burglars, robbers and molesters, the feebleminded and intelligent. Each was welcomed in the same way behind the impregnable walls built of limestone hewed from the institutional quarry, and each yielded to a regimen calculated to make the inmate feel that he was "nothing much more above the beast."

Red's rite of passage began with the warden, who, after a brief interview, sent his latest guest along to the department of the chief keeper, where the young prisoner's measurements and physical characteristics were recorded and what remained of his personal possessions, inventoried. He was then bathed, shaved, shorn of his hair, and awarded a red-and-white-checked uniform with a number stamped on the back of the coat.

Banished to his cell, Red lapsed into a dismal routine. He rose at 6:30 in the morning, washed, made his bed, and, at 7:00 marched to the kitchen for breakfast, where servers dropped gobs of watered porridge onto tin plates as the men filed by. Breakfast was eaten in the cell with a spoon; knives and forks were forbidden. On the way to work, the dishes were returned to the kitchen. Similar routines applied to dinner and supper, both eaten alone in the cell, where the prisoners remained until the following morning.

Kingston's prison system rested on the twin pillars of silence and isolation. An inmate was not allowed to speak to officers or fellow convicts "except from necessity or with respect to his work." "In his cell," a royal commission reported, "he is not allowed pictures or photographs of his relatives, he is not allowed to have or read a newspaper but he is furnished books from the prison library. If he is unable to read, he must put in fourteen hours of each day alone, sleeping or meditating. On Sunday, the whole day — with the exception of one hour for Divine Service — is spent in the cells and when a holiday falls on Monday, he celebrates it with an additional twenty-four hours of solitary confinement."

The Portsmouth prison was plainly no reclamation center, and Red Ryan, among the youngest of the prisoners there, received little encouragement or training to help him abandon a career of crime inspired, he later wrote, by "an adventurous disposition and a distorted, vain desire for leadership." If, as the learned commissioners inquiring into penitentiary conditions noted, the years sixteen to twenty-one were "crucial years in the formation of character," then Ryan's Kingston visit served only one purpose — to reinforce and harden the infirmities which had brought him there. Kingston's warden made no pretense of educating the prisoners, young or old, keen or dull. "The indifferent attempts to improve the illiterate at Kingston Penitentiary," the commissioners reported, "can scarcely be dignified by the name of school." Half an hour to forty minutes a day, four days a week, were set aside for instruction. Nor did the prison workshops impart skills to the inmate or inspire a positive attitude to work. "The industrial conditions in the penitentiaries of Canada," the commissioners noted, "are a disgrace to the Dominion. . . . There is not a single well-equipped well-managed, continuously busy shop in the whole circle of prisons." According to J. A. Edmison, Q.C., later a member of Canada's National Parole Board, at the time of Ryan's admission to Kingston Penitentiary "there was no prison psychiatrist, no psychologist, no classification officer, no educational courses or trade training worth the name." Particularly abhorrent was the stone-breaking shop, where Red was assigned, his legs weighted with thirty-five-pound Oregon boots designed to prevent escape. Over seventy prisoners were at work in the shop when a group of royal commissioners appeared during Ryan's prison tenure. "They were arranged in rows facing each other," the commissioners observed, "and the stone to be broken was piled in a long heap between them. As the raw material was reduced to the required size, fresh supplies were wheeled in by tenders from the yard. There was perfect order among them. Not a word was spoken. But the monotonous rap of the hammers, the sullen whitened faces of the forms, half crouching over their unhealthy, unprofitable, degrading task, were a mute but powerful denunciation of the system that permitted, or rendered necessary, such an outrage. Nothing has been said, nothing can be said, in defence of this twentieth century reproduction of the unceasing toil of the galley slave."

Red Ryan learned no new and useful trade in the penitentiary workshops, but he did serve an apprenticeship, of sorts, in a school for crime. "While there," he later reminisced, "we associated with hardened criminals, some of the most vicious types, and all we heard while in prison was boasting about the 'jobs' they had pulled and what they planned to do in all channels of crime when they got out." From this prep school, Red graduated with honors on September 24, 1914, on a ticket of leave for good behavior, on condition that he return home and place himself under the care of his father, who had advised the Justice Department that a place could be made for his son in the family tinsmithing business. Just as Red had entered a poor boy, so did he leave impoverished, his sole assets, aside from his personal effects, being $4.95 — the $5.00 prison allowance less five cents deducted for a carfare on the streetcar line connecting Portsmouth to the railway station in Kingston.

Red was determined, however, to make up for lost time and income and on the very day of his release met with a fellow parolee to plan ways of doing so. They soon embarked on a series of armed holdups involving the Dominion Express Company in Parkdale and, on April 15, 1915, the payroll office of the Toronto Piano Factory, where Red had worked while a schoolboy.

Following the piano factory holdup, Ryan and his friend visited Owen Sound where they stole a motorcycle in preparation for a bank heist. Local police, however, spotted them on the stolen machine and, after a lengthy pursuit across a lake, succeeded in wounding Ryan and capturing the pair. On June 16, 1915, in the city of Owen Sound, Red was sentenced to eight years in the Kingston Penitentiary. Several months later, he was removed from his cell to Toronto and there charged with robbery with violence for the piano factory and Dominion Express holdups. A further twenty-four years — twelve on each charge — were added to his sentence.

Red Ryan's brief, and largely petty, criminal career seemed all but ended. On returning to his Portsmouth home, Red was greeted by familiar faces and fell into old ways. The warden advised him to be a good boy and behave. The chief keeper arranged for his clothing, numbering, and haircut. The custodial officers saw to it that his daily route from cell to kitchen, workshop, and back again was traced without incident.

Red performed sensibly for over two and one-half years, until events outside the walls of the penitentiary and outside the Dominion of Canada — in the European War theater — kindled his hopes for freedom. The Great War had drained Canada's manpower overseas, where a rising casualty rate moved the Dominion government to adopt a policy of registration and conscription of manpower. By 1918, the situation had become so critical that the federal authorities desperately began to scour society's hidden crevices, including the penitentiaries, for recruits.

It is unlikely that Red Ryan was attracted to a military vocation, just as he had never seriously entertained the notion of pursuing a career of industrial labor. Red's love of adventure and quick gain precluded him from settling into routine wage employment or submitting to the discipline of military authority. He much preferred criminals to corporals, and gangs to platoons. Enlistment for service, however, did have a certain attraction; it was a ticket of leave from the dreaded penitentiary. Accordingly, on March 26, 1918, Red Ryan waved goodbye to Portsmouth for a second time, after serving two years and nine months of his sentence.

Canada's Princess Pat's had gained a dubious recruit, who, instead of rushing to the front, deserted to the rear soon after arriving in England. Deprived of His Majesty's pay and provisions, Red stole from army stores and, in October, 1918, was caught and sentenced to six weeks imprisonment. After serving time in the army lockup at Seaford in Sussex and at Whitley camp, which he abandoned through a skylight, Red Ryan deserted England, the army, and the pursuing police and embarked on a sea voyage with the merchant navy to places unknown. But, in early 1921, under the alias of Albert Slade — a name he borrowed from a vanished sailor — he returned to his native Toronto and there renewed some old acquaintances.

Like other veterans, Red Ryan did not adjust easily to the economic chaos of postwar Canada. Finding it hard to "steady down to work" in Toronto, he sought economic opportunity elsewhere. "In the spring of 1921, I went to Hamilton, Ontario," he recalled, "and spent a great deal of time around there in a club where I met a great many fine fellows." During the summer he married a "fine little girl" at Saint Peter's Church, Toronto, returned to Hamilton, and began "sizing up the various branch banks for a lay that appealed to me." Red found a branch of the Bank of Hamilton to his liking but was driven away by the manager in a bungled robbery attempt. The next day, however, he appeared alone at the Locke and Main Street branch of the Union Bank and robbed it of five thousand dollars.

The "swag" yielded some good times. "I liked Hamilton," Red admitted, "and was having a fine time around a little bungalow down in the Delta district where I can truthfully say that I met a fine bunch of fellows. There was a little good beer and we had some sociable times there. . . ." But the easy fun and big money soon dissipated, and several weeks after the Union Bank heist, Red Ryan, known for a while as "Texas Bell," decided to try his luck again, this time at the Locke and Herkimer branch of the Bank of Hamilton.

By now, Red had established a workable routine. He visited the bank, observed the layout, and noted the number and distribution of employees. More importantly, he studied the surrounding area. "The actual game of knocking them down is the easy part of it," he later explained, "but it is the getaway that counts." To facilitate the flight, he and a partner, George McVittie — the latter using the alias Patrick O'Hara — stole an old Ford touring automobile several hours before Red's appearance at the door of the bank, ten minutes before the 3:00 P.M. closing time.

Dressed in a shabby suit, battered brown boots, and a peaked brown cap that shielded his face, Red walked swiftly over to the teller's cage, pointed the blue muzzle of his revolver into the face of the teller-manager, a Mr. Chester Gibson, and said, "Hands up and keep 'em up! No kidding — I mean business." Mr. Gibson obeyed, as did his ledger keeper beside him, a Mr. Marshall. A junior clerk nearby, however, bolted for the side door and was intercepted by Ryan, who leaped the counter, lined the employees up against the wall near the vault, and scooped cash, bills, and silver totaling around $3,800 from the teller's cage. Just then, a woman entered the bank and was ordered by Ryan to sit quietly. Red secured the manager's revolver from the cage, frisked the other employees, and tapped Mr. Gibson playfully with his gun before inquiring where other money and bonds might be. Mr. Gibson's word, that the vault held nothing, was accepted, and Ryan left through a side door. "There is a thrill when you have the swag," he later recounted, "but you can never tell when they may get you in the back. I made my waiting limousine and returned downtown and parked the car in the centre of the city, and went and cut up the melon."

In the next few days, Ryan and McVittie's exploits attracted such intensive police and media attention that they decided, after a visit to the race track to change and lose money, to leave Hamilton. With their funds running low, the bandits headed for Montreal, where, in late October, they assaulted the Park Avenue and Prince Arthur branch of the Bank of Commerce. But Red ran into trouble when the manager, usually absent during the lunchhour break, seized a gun from his desk drawer and fired at Ryan, who was covering the teller and ledger keeper with an automatic revolver in each hand. The shots missed, as did the return fire of the bandit, who let go simultaneously from both guns. All of this caused Mr. G. T. Drew, the teller, to faint, and the bandits, after firing another round in the manager's direction, to vacate to their stolen car.

The Ontario invaders retreated to their hideaway, the central Y.M.C.A. on Drummond Street where, two days later, they were ambushed by a pair of detectives, as they stepped outside. A wild shoot-out resulted in the arrest of both and the subsequent conviction of Red Ryan on December 9, 1921, on charges of robbery with violence and shooting with intent to kill. He was sentenced to seven years and forty lashes in the Saint Vincent de Paul Penitentiary. After serving a portion of the sentence and taking the lashes, Red was removed to Hamilton where he stood trial on bank holdup charges. The young man, described by Chief Dickson of the Toronto police force as a "vicious, dangerous and resourceful thief," was found guilty of robbing two banks, of attempting to rob a third, and of shooting with intent to kill. He was given twenty-five years, while McVittie was found guilty of robbing one bank and was sentenced to ten years.

Had Red Ryan, upon his third entry into Kingston Penitentiary, been decrepit or dealt a shorter term or been somehow convinced of the justice of his sentence, he might have resigned himself to a lengthy term of penal servitude. But Red was still a young man, lean and energetic, whose sense of fair play had been offended by the length of his penalty as compared to that received by his confederate McVittie. "If I had got ten years," he protested, "I would have tried for my good conduct time, but when a man as young as I was, and not aged by my recent troubles, has such a long confinement ahead of him, it is a great temptation to make a break." From the moment of his return to prison, Red Ryan thought of little else but escaping; an obsession that, in the autumn of 1923, took on concrete form.

To leave Kingston's grimy fortress without Warden J. C. Ponsford's official blessing was no simple matter, and Ryan, after careful screening, enlisted a formidable gang of confederates in an escape plot: Arthur (Curly) Sullivan, alias Brown, a Toronto east-end boy specializing in west-end robberies, who was caught in a rooming house melting down stolen silverware and sentenced to a ten-year term; Gordon Simpson, also a Toronto thief, convicted of a series of robberies in Hamilton, Toronto, and Guelph; Thomas (Runty) Bryans, a twenty-one year old from Sault Sainte Marie, jailed on a manslaughter charge; and Edward (Wyoming) McMullen, a gangster with a lengthy record, described by Kingston Penitentiary's deputy warden, R. H. Tucker, as "cold as ice, silent, unmovable as a gypsy's curse," serving twenty-four years for the robbery of a bank in Wyoming, Ontario.

The escape plot, hatched after two months of preparation, centered on the prison's east wall where, at midmorning on September 10, 1923, an elderly prisoner, charged with supervisory duties in the barn area, was suddenly seized and bound by several inmates, who promptly set fire to a

THE SAGA OF RED RYAN

large strawstack. Under cover of a thick screen of yellow-gray smoke, which, wafted by a favorable wind, obscured the wall area from the view of the watchtower guards, five convicts dressed in gray prison garb raced from the barn towards the east wall. The lead man carried a long two-by-four, fitted at intervals with large spikes, which he leaned against the twenty-foot wall. Arthur Sullivan went up first, carrying a rope, which, attached to the scaffolding above, carried him down the other side. While Red stood guard at the bottom of the ladder, his confederates scrambled up and over in a matter of seconds. Ryan followed but had only taken a step or two when the chief keeper, Matt Walsh, arrived and began shaking the ladder. After jumping to the ground, Ryan grabbed a pitchfork, laid nearby for just such an emergency, and wrestled and clubbed the keeper to the ground. He then joined his colleagues in a wild dash towards the property of millionaire H. W. Richardson, which adjoined the prison.

The convicts hoped that the Richardson family would be home so that they could enlist the services of their high-powered automobile. But the house was vacant and there was no car on the premises except a battered little Chevrolet, owned by Mr. "Shorty" Thompson, a painter employed to touch up the Richardson mansion. The convicts seized the car and, with McMullen at the wheel, sped away in a hail of bullets fired by pursuing guards, who succeeded in wounding McMullen in the hand. The prison guards, in a battered Ford, were joined by a force of police and volunteers, who, in a fleet of twenty commandeered cars, chased the convicts through the streets of Kingston, then east of town along a stone county road, past a quarry, across two sets of railway tracks, and down a long, steep hill. The convicts' lead was no more than two hundred yards when McMullen, weak from loss of blood, lost control of the wheel and ran the car down an embankment and into a farmer's gate, about three miles from Kingston. The car was abandoned and its frantic inhabitants fled into the adjoining seven hundred acres of woods and swamp.

It did not take the guards long to capture the dazed Edward McMullen, who was found sprawled on the ground near the bottom of a fence, with his blue shirt drawn over his head, only a hundred yards from the abandoned car. It was no easy matter, however, locating the other escapees in the vast forest known as Kemp's and McAdoo's woods, where sixty guards were soon joined by a mounted police party from the Royal Canadian Horse Artillery and by a force of provincial policemen.

Red Ryan and his friends spent a desperate few days foraging for food, drinking slough water, dodging guards and police, stealing from local farmhouses, and slashing through brush on a hike that took them several miles from their abandoned car. Throughout their frantic vigil, they managed to keep near a road that ran through their wooded sanctuary and, when the opportunity presented itself, approximately twelve miles from Campbelltown, they stole a car and headed for Toronto. "On the fourth night of our escape," Ryan later recalled, "we blew into the city of Toronto. . . . We were still in our prison uniforms and went riding through the centre of the city, avoiding accidents and crossings where we would be held up. Down one of the main streets of Toronto, we came to our destination. We got into that house quick, and we all slept well in the coal bin."

During the next few days, the convicts renewed old contacts, changed houses and clothing, kept indoors at daytime, and amused themselves reading press accounts of the police searches. But they were pressed for funds and soon planned a withdrawal from the Oakwood-Saint Clair branch of the Bank of Nova Scotia, whose very vault, Ryan later admitted, he had lined years earlier while working as a tinsmith.

The operation began with the removal of license plates from a wrecked car. Then, on the morning of September 27, an Overland car owned by a Dr. F. A. Clarkson, disappeared from in front of the Western Hospital on Bathurst Street. After switching plates at the Stanley Barracks, the gang drove to Biggar Street, a block from the bank, where the car was parked and the neighborhood "cased." Sullivan visited the bank to change a twenty-dollar bill and check the layout. Soon afterwards, around 1:15 P.M., the convicts entered the bank and drew their guns. Simpson presented himself at the office door of the manager, a Mr. Leroy Oake, who, slow to respond to a request to open the vault, was clubbed unconscious with the butt of a gun. While Sullivan guarded the door and kept several customers at bay, Red Ryan leaped the counter, ordered the teller and several clerks into the manager's office, ripped the phone out, and filled a canvas bag with cash — around three thousand dollars — from the drawers in the teller's cage. Pursued by an awakened and aroused manager, who fired several shots, and by a pack of students from the nearby Oakwood Collegiate, the gang returned to their waiting car, tracing a zigzag route through the streets of downtown Toronto. Dr. Clarkson's Overland was abandoned next day in the parking lot of the Granite Club on Church Street.

The police, the public, the sore-headed Mr. Leroy Oake knew who had pulled the job and, in the days and weeks following, imputed a host of like efforts to the Kingston Four. "With an audacious daylight hold-up in Toronto on Thursday," the *Toronto Daily Star* reported, "a safe cracked in Hamilton and 15,000 dollars in cash stolen on Sunday, a post office robbed in Queenston on Monday, a taxicab driver relieved of his car, driver's licence, cash and watch near St. Catharines on the same day, and the description of the criminals who escaped from Kingston Penitentiary agreeing in some respects with those given for the perpetrators of these crimes, a path of violence and banditry seems to be moving westward across the province . . . and naturally, suspicion falls on the convicts."

While the criminal wave diffused westward from Kingston, Red Ryan and his colleagues escaped south towards the American border. Soon after the Oakwood-Saint Clair holdup, Ryan and Sullivan split from their confederates, picked up "a real machine, the fastest thing on wheels," and, in the company of several friends, departed for Windsor. Outside London, near a town called Pottersburg, they stopped in the evening at a closed service station and were helping themselves to oil when a motorcycle policeman pulled into the station. While Ryan readied his gun for firing through the rear curtain of the car, Sullivan, who had emptied the oil can outside, explained that they were tourists in a hurry and were prepared to leave a five-dollar bill for the oil. The constable bought their story, according to Ryan, and was kind enough to escort them four or five miles towards the Sarnia road.

Armed to the teeth, with saws and other escape gadgets sewn into the seams of their clothing in the event of capture, Ryan and Sullivan drove to the Saint Clair River near Windsor and, at Sombra, hitched a ride in a bootlegger's launch across to the American side. They bought a car in Detroit, where police were deemed too vigilant due to a recent epidemic of holdups, and drove to Chicago, also apparently too well policed for their liking. They finally settled for Minnesota's twin cities, Saint Paul and Minneapolis, as a good place to rest awhile and plot their moves.

Ryan later recalled that he enjoyed Minneapolis, where he dyed his hair black and met some nice, decent people, among them a tall, slender, and blonde waitress employed by the Minneapolis Athletic Club, whom Sullivan dated. "I met Ryan and Brown (Sullivan) early in November," Miss Irene Adams recounted; "they were well-dressed, pleasant and certainly spent money like water. They told me they were automobile accessory salesmen. Shortly after I met them, they went on a trip to New York, Philadelphia, Boston and other eastern cities. They sent me postcards everywhere they went." The travels of "the Miller brothers," as they were known, yielded some good hauls, including a short jaunt to neighboring Saint Paul where the Grant Avenue State Bank was relieved of five thousand dollars in early November.

Although the Miller brothers ranged as far afield as Flint, Michigan and Boston, Massachusetts in the east, and Fargo, North Dakota in the Midwest, they rarely lost contact with their Canadian families and friends with whom they maintained a lively, and sometimes unorthodox, correspondence. Red had the temerity to use an American police publication, known as *The Detective* — an official journal printed in Chicago and used by police and sheriffs in the United States to advertise for fugitives from justice — to keep in touch with friends. By previous arrangement, special coded personal ads were inserted, notifying the parties concerned of addresses and pickup points.

The Toronto police knew nothing at the time about this scandalous practice, but, through contact with a Toronto woman whom Red corresponded with, they did learn, in early December, about the fugitive's Minneapolis location and habit of claiming mail at the general-delivery window of the main post office. The source of the tip was reliable enough to send Mr. R. H. Tucker, deputy warden of the Kingston Penitentiary, and Mr. Walter Duncan, chief of the criminal investigation branch of the federal Department of Justice and a former Toronto police chief, who had recently been assigned to the case, on a hurried mission to Minneapolis, where they consulted earnestly with the local police.

On the evening of Friday, December 15, while Messrs. Tucker and Duncan waited nervously nearby at their operations headquarters in the Hotel Radisson, Red Ryan entered the central post office and walked over to the general-delivery wicket to collect his mail. Just as he reached the window, he noticed a stocky gentleman next to him in rough clothes whom he took, correctly, to be a detective. Ryan and Maxon, the Minneapolis officer, went for their guns simultaneously and each succeeded in firing past the other. But a third shot, from a colleague of Maxon's who had approached from the other side, hit Red in the right shoulder, half spun him around, and caused him to drop his gun.

Offering no further resistance, Red was manacled and rushed into the street where several other detectives were stationed nearby. But as he walked through the door, Red shouted across the street towards a waiting car, from which Curly Sullivan opened fire, injuring a policeman and several bystanders. Sullivan took some return fire and received a nick in the nose, not severe enough, however, to deter him from keeping a theater and supper appointment with Miss Irene Adams following his escape down a side street. "He was right on the dot," Miss Adams noted; "he seemed cool and collected, but held a handkerchief to his nose. He said his nose had been bleeding."

The next day Miss Adams received a pair of visitors, Messrs. Meehan and Forbes of the Minneapolis police force, who waited around her apartment after Sullivan phoned to announce an early afternoon visit. Meehan took no chances when the bandit arrived. "I will never forget that wait for him to rap at the door," Miss Adams stated; "when we heard him coming, the detectives told me to get out, but I saw him open the door. As he saw the detectives in the room, he started to pull his revolver. Detective Meehan shot over Detective Forbes' shoulder and Brown fell across the doorway. It was horrible. But the detectives were as cold as ice.

69

Detective Forbes said: 'Nice work, Bill,' and that was all they said. . . . Believe me, I moved out of that room in a hurry. I could never sleep there another night. This was a lesson for me. I will select my friends more carefully in the future."

The body of Curly Sullivan, killed by a single shot through the heart, was removed to the local morgue and later identified by his jailed colleague. It was Detective Meehan — fiftyish, squat, hardened — who broke the news, after walking into Red's cell and asking casually, "How are you?" When Ryan replied, "Much better," Meehan assured him he would soon have a chance to see his partner. "Got him downstairs?" Ryan asked. "No," Meehan responded, "at the morgue."

Red Ryan was shaken at the sight of Sullivan on the slab, and when the dead man's wife arrived to claim the body, he asked for and was granted permission to speak privately with her. When press reports appeared in Minneapolis and Toronto alleging that Red Ryan had a yellow streak and had betrayed his friend by disclosing Miss Adams's address to the police, Ryan heatedly denied the charge, a disclaimer supported by Chief Walter Duncan, who later stated that other sources had revealed Sullivan's whereabouts. Red volunteered the opinion that Curly's demise had followed from his failure to obey the fugitives' imperative never to confide in or consort with "skirts" while on the run.

In any event, what Red Ryan contemplated in the frosty days and nights preceding Christmas, 1923, was a fate as bad as, or worse than, Curly Sullivan's. Banished to a chilly cell, the Jesse James of Canada, as the Hearst press called him, shivered and complained about the cold until his jailers yielded to his request for an overcoat. Hidden in the lining was a file, which Red applied to the bars at night, every night, for nineteen days while the lawyers and authorities — American and Canadian; state, federal, and provincial — exchanged papers involving extradition, bail, and sundry matters. Red made decent progress and succeeded in sawing through a pair of bars. From strips of his blanket, sheets, and clothing, including a blood-stained undershirt, he assembled a twenty-foot ladder, long enough to drop him to the fourth-floor hallway, which led down several stairways and past a single guard to the streets outside.

But the wheels of justice moved too quickly. When Chief Brunskill arrived at Red's cell one day to announce his removal to the county jail pending extradition, he was greeted with excitement and consternation. After searching Red's cell, the chief discovered why. Brunskill, it turned out, was pleased to rid himself of the multinational bandit. "Ryan was by far the toughest and most desperate man ever held in our jail," the chief declared following a testimonial banquet given in his honor by civic leaders at the exclusive Minneapolis Club. In the presence of Messrs. Tucker, Duncan, and Meehan, all guests of honor, Brunskill was presented with a silver trophy — which subsequently held a place of pride on his desk at headquarters — inscribed with the names of the officers, dates and brief facts concerning the capture of the notorious Canadian bandit.

While Chief Brunskill warmed to his trophy, Red Ryan's hands were cuffed, his feet shackled, and body removed, in the company of Meehan, Maxon, Duncan, and Tucker, in the early evening of Friday, January 14, by train to Toronto. The party switched trains in twenty-eight-below-zero (Fahrenheit) weather at Blind River, Ontario, where a *Star* reporter joined the entourage and sent back detailed accounts, headlined on the front pages, of Red's thoughts and moods. During stops in west Toronto and at Union Station, the party of Red's guards was augmented by contingents of plainclothesmen and Toronto city police until it swelled to fourteen.

The elaborate security seemed unnecessary. The man who arrived at Union Station could barely move. His hands were trussed "like the drumsticks of a Christmas turkey," a reporter observed, "and his legs were so tightly bound that he could move only in short hops." Dressed in a light fawn overcoat, tightly buckled at the waist, with a neat round hole, blackened at the edges, visible on his right shoulder, Ryan's homecoming was, according to a reporter for the *Star* (which devoted a full, lurid page to his return), "as commonplace as the delivery of a package by a postman." Even Red's legendary hair and fabled freckles seemed to have faded. "He may be as black as painted," a reporter observed, "but he's not nearly so red. His hair is like lustreless sand. His face has the sallowness of long-effaced freckles. In fact, he's not red at all and should be called Sandy Ryan and not Red Ryan."

Red, however, did not care much about appearances or the attendant surge of publicity that moved the board of directors of the Big Brothers movement and the Toronto Presbytery to protest the excessive prominence given in the press to prison escapes, as tending to "glorify crime and criminals."[1] Nor was he troubled by a *Star* editorialist who reminded his readers that "an ordinary labourer gets more real pleasure out of life" than a criminal, or by the aroused executive of the Women's Christian

---

1. *Toronto Daily Star*, January 10, 1924. In an editorial entitled "The Penalties of Crime," the *Star* wrote: "It is a pity that the daily life of a criminal, in prison or out of it, could not be described and read; but the difficulty is that it would be so sordid and dreary that the greatest artist in words could not tell the story in such a way to hold the attention of the reader. The Ryan sentence is hardly less to be feared than death but even where light sentences are imposed the criminal career alternates between terms of imprisonment and a precarious and anxious existence in the outside world. An unskilled labourer gets more real pleasure out of life."

Red Ryan (center) back in Toronto in January, 1924, to face charges.

Temperance Union who, reacting to a report that a Red Ryan autobiography would soon be published, petitioned the Department of Justice in order to "prevent the publication, circulation and sale of any book or work emanating from the pen of that notorious criminal called Red Ryan." Red wanted matters over and done with quickly and decided to plead guilty to the Bank of Nova Scotia charge. His trial, before Judge Emerson Coatsworth, lasted a brief two hours and heard Crown Attorney Armour deplore the recent sensational publicity. "Certain newspapers have seen fit to picture him as a glorified hero," Armour told the court, "whereas the fact is, he is a vulgar criminal." Red's own counsel, Mr. Austin Ross, asked for mercy on the grounds that his client was "a pitiable object today. His career is over. He knows now that there is nothing in a life of crime. He is a broken man." Judge Coatsworth awarded Ryan life imprisonment and thirty strokes of the lash to be administered ten a month for the first three months.

Red's return was a big event in Kingston, where, in the wintry evening of January 8, 1928, several hundred people crowded the railway tracks to catch a glimpse of the captive outlaw. Among them was Warden Ponsford and a troupe of guards, who cleared an aisle to the automobile that had sped Ryan, a pair of detectives, and Messrs. Duncan and Tucker, to the prison gates. In the registration room, Red sat on a bench while Warden Ponsford and Deputy Warden Tucker shook his hand and exchanged greetings, and Inspector Duncan removed the shackles and handcuffs, which were neatly folded and dropped into a grip. Red then exchanged his clothes for a prison uniform, after submitting to an inspection that probed the very hairs of his head and soles of his feet.

Because he had caused Warden Ponsford all that fuss and bother, Red was granted, on his return, a special status and residency — in a long stone building next to the chief keeper's office, which ran north and south along the east wall and was known as the prison of isolation, an institution devoted to keeping the damned and incorrigibles in a state of solitary confinement. It was here, in the Hole, in an underground cell along one of the prison's six corridors, that Red was kept for the first nine months after his return, in a state of almost total isolation. The cell windows were painted over in white, blocking any view of the outside. A board served as a bed and meals were taken in the cell. He was denied access to the workshop and exercise yard. One day, according to Ryan, he almost died after gulping from a bottle of ammonia mistakenly given him by a guard in place of medicine. His main companions were mice, guards, and books.

There were several important visitors during Red's dungeon days. Warden Ponsford appeared one morning, noted Red's assurance that he would never try to escape again, and offered words of encouragement. The kindly Reverend Father Wilfred T. Kingsley, the Roman Catholic chaplain of the penitentiary and parish priest at Portsmouth's Church of the Good Thief, also visited and advised Red to forget the past, study the Bible, and devote himself to the single task of reformation. It was on Father Kingsley's recommendation that Red was moved, after nine months in the Hole, to a cell in another wing of the prison of isolation where he spent a further year and a half. Not until the final sixty days was he allowed, under special guard, into the yard for twenty minutes of exercise per day in the open air.

Red's solitary confinement had a chastening effect. "Because I was in solitary, I didn't work like the other convicts," he later wrote, "and I had plenty of time to read . . . as I always had a Bible beside me in my cell, I took to reading it to pass the time away. It was then I first cultivated a taste for literature. I read the Bible purely as a narrative of history but subconsciously, I have no doubt, its splendid passages helped crystalize my purpose to reform." Red's reading — of books and his own dreary life history; his subjection to the ultimate punishment of lonely confinement; and the kind encouragements of Father Kingsley, his spiritual adviser, moved him, during the dark months of isolation, to transcend despair and contemplate a full reformation of his life. "There were times during the early days of my solitary confinement," he continued, "when I all but gave up hope of ever carrying through my determination to reform. I had no contact with any humans except the prison staff. . . . I hadn't heard from my wife. . . . Sometimes in black moods of despair, I wondered if I wasn't embarked on a useless struggle that couldn't get me anywhere. But always the realization of the faith of others held in me and the recognition of the hopelessness in store for anyone who gives himself over to outlawry, brought me out of my despondency. I got a new grip on myself and began to take a real joy out of my ambition to make good, no matter how tough the road."

The new Red Ryan did not go unnoticed by Warden Ponsford, who, early in 1926, relocated him into the mailbag department, which provided the Dominion postal service with a fresh supply of new and repaired bags. Here Red put his tinsmith training to good use and busied himself for two years with fixing labels, repairing metal parts, and other chores. It was reported in *The Globe* in November, 1926, that Red had invented a theft-proof lock for mailbags — subsequently adopted for use by the postal service — so cleverly constructed that he himself was unable to pick it open.[2]

For his dedicated postal service, Red earned a further promotion in 1928: to the coveted post of nurse in the prison hospital, where living conditions were better than any in the institution and senior inmate employees could, relatively speaking, come and go as they pleased. At first, as a junior nurse, Red was required to return to his cell at night while assisting the noisy and unpopular head orderly known to the prison fraternity as the Bull of Basham. Red suffered under the autocracy of the Bull, whose subsequent parole created a senior vacancy that Red was pleased to fill.

It took six long years for Red Ryan to rise from the desolation of the dungeon floor to the rank of head orderly nurse in the hospital, the

---

2. Stories circulating that Ryan's relatives were living in ease off royalties from the lock were found by a *Star* reporter to be untrue. Ryan's application for a patent, made in March, 1929, had lapsed and was forfeited through nonpayment of a fee. A spokesman for the post office confirmed that a lock had been invented by Ryan, considered for use, and rejected.

highest inmate position in the penitentiary. As head orderly, he inherited large responsibilities. He ministered to patients; fed, massaged, and nursed them; took their temperatures; supplied friends in need (like Edward McMullen) with six ounces of alcohol twice weekly; and assisted the doctors in their operations, minor and major. "He is as tender as any female nurse in his treatment of the sick men confided to his care," Dr. O. J. Withrow, a prison inmate, observed; "by his great strength, he lifts them easily when he wills." When the jailed Communist leader, Tim Buck, was operated on, Red assisted the surgeon, Professor Austin of Queen's University, and noted that "Buck was the most stoical patient I think I ever saw in the hospital. He took everything as stoically as Socrates." Buck, it seems, proved more compliant than a fellow inmate who fell under Ryan's ministrations. "A little while ago, I had occasion to rub the chest of a Jew with alcohol," Red later recounted. "He was rather an annoying patient and peevishly complained that he felt chilly. I told him he would soon warm up when the alcohol took hold. He didn't become any warmer for all my rubbing and I was astonished to find, when I looked at the bottle, that I had been using Holy Water."

For his good work, Red was granted special privileges. On his promotion to head orderly, he relocated into a room in the upper ward of the hospital, where he moved about as he pleased and escaped the routine of the cell block. Meals and sanitary conditions improved, and his room, decorated with pictures and an assortment of books, was comfortably furnished with a cot, mattress, table, and gramophone. "He had the free run of the hospital," Buck observed; "this I can vouch for because I was in the hospital myself for a while. While I was supposed to be behind steel gates, which were locked and opened only for the bringing in of meals, Red used to bring me a cup of tea and fresh cream at 11 o'clock in the morning, and again at 4 o'clock in the afternoon. He used to bring me little bits of cake from the officers mess and, as I was getting better, he would ask me if I would like a little 'snifter.' He used to go in and out any time he wanted; he had the keys."

Red's elevation by the administration was commensurate with his status among the prisoners. In the inverted world of the prison, the violent bank bandit stood highest both among his peers and, apparently, the authorities, who absorbed him into their administrative apparatus. According to Buck, "Everything was upside down in the penitentiary. A boy, who in a moment of deviltry, had stolen a car to go for a joy ride and who had been sentenced to two years plus one day, and another boy, only sixteen, who had stolen a pair of shoes and had been sentenced to three years — these were the lowest down the ladder. The fellows who were the elite were the men who used guns, stick-up men, especially those who had robbed or attempted to rob a bank. Red Ryan was top in every respect because of his reputation. Even the administration treated him in a special way."

Had Red Ryan been a difficult inmate, he would have received — his prestigious stickup status notwithstanding — no special treatment from Warden Ponsford, except, of course, of the punitive sort. But Red proved himself, year in and year out, a "model prisoner." A trim, muscular six-footer, with alert, intelligent eyes, and a charming easy manner, Red never looked the part of the ugly thug, the grotesque enemy of society. "He was as different from the newspaper or storybook criminal," Dr. Withrow wrote, "as the rosy dawn differs from the blackness of midnight. I am reminded of the description of David of sacred history, 'now he was ruddy and withall of a beautiful countenance and goodly to look to.' " Nor did he play the role of rebel during one of the worst periods of unrest in Kingston's history. During the several riots that occurred during his tenure — including a serious outbreak in 1933 — he prudently kept clear of the field of action. "Known to all the inmates as a two-fisted he-man without a streak of yellow," Father Kingsley observed following the 1933 riots, "his co-operation, not to say leadership, would have been invaluable; they received neither."

Red more than avoided trouble. He performed good, merciful work in the hospital and aided Father Kingsley in his ministrations to the fallen flock. The new Red Ryan abstained from smoking and blasphemy, served as an altar boy during church services, built miniature crucifixes inside light bulbs, and moulded images of the Virgin Mary. According to Dr. Withrow, who became a close prison friend of Ryan, the chaplain looked upon Red as his curate, who saw to it "that none of the religious rites of their faith are neglected by the Roman Catholic patients." When a new archbishop visited the prison during Sunday services, Red was chosen by his coreligionists to deliver the welcoming address.

All of this, Red performed with such evident sincerity that Father Kingsley, no mushy sentimentalist, was moved to commence with others a campaign for Red's release on a ticket of leave. Although Red was hidden from public view for almost a decade by Portsmouth's gray anonymity, he was not without friends, family, and interested publicists outside, who shared Father Kingsley's views that he had atoned for his sins and was ready to return to normal and productive life in civil society. Since his spectacular flight from the penitentiary and his equally newsworthy capture, Red had become a favorite of the metropolitan Toronto press, both the *Star* and the *Globe*, whose accounts of his moral progress were picked up by other newspapers across the country. A steady trickle of articles appeared in the late 1920s, about Red's invention of the mail lock; about his cache of twenty thousand dollars, which the *Ottawa Journal* reported he set aside to help his tubercular

Red Ryan (left), Father Kingsley (right).

sister; about his kindly medical ministrations, headlined in a *Mail* story "Famous bandit proves tender nurse in prison." Early in 1932, a front-page feature article appeared in the *Star*, quoting former inmates who described Ryan as "a man completely reformed." A *Star* "representative" who interviewed Ryan, heard that he wanted to "carry a dinner pail" if released or establish a little shop, cigar store, or a haberdashery in Kingston, "close enough to the prison so that all my friends, the guards and the officials of the Warden's office could come and visit me regularly." Ryan, it was further disclosed, had developed an interest in Einstein's theory of relativity and in the intricacies of international trade and world currency problems. His business acumen was appreciated by four imprisoned stock brokers, who professed their eagerness to employ him once he and they, prospective employers and employee, obtained their release. When Dr. Withrow was released from

77

Kingston penitentiary and wrote a series of articles for the *Globe* in 1933, exposing life and conditions in the "Big House," he devoted an entire article to his friend whom he considered "kind-hearted, conscientious, loyal, innately honest and big-souled, whose only desire was to do the right thing in a big way if he is permitted."

Dr. Withrow's views were endorsed, if less enthusiastically, by others including Red's brother Russell, who bombarded the press and government and prison officials with supplicatory missives, including copies of letters to him by Red, penned in a neat hand, impeccably grammared, and laced with quotations, professing new ways and moral commitments. But the true architect of the campaign for release was Father Kingsley, Red's friend, confidant, and spiritual adviser, who assured the parole board, in a letter written in December, 1933, that he was willing to take Ryan into his home "under any conditions that the Department may impose and keep him as long as they desired, I can give no greater testimony of my regard for Ryan." Father Kingsley noted that Ryan, despite his lurid career, had never taken a life, had served a notable portion of his sentence, had abstained from all prison disturbances and had exhibited "exemplary conduct" (he lost three days on a single report for talking). He was convinced that Ryan's release would have a positive moral effect: "It will stimulate eagerness to obey the rules; there will be something more than a desire to avoid punishment; from the depair of 'what's the use,' there will rise the constant hope of 'there is every use, see Ryan.' "

Father Kingsley's representations were supported by others. When Judge Emerson Coatsworth, who had sentenced Ryan to his life term, heard a Toronto lawyer refer to Ryan in court as "a hardened criminal," he rebuked him and explained "that Red Ryan had become a very estimable citizen." A North Bay judge thought that, upon his release, Ryan should be given a job lecturing to wayward boys in reformatories, while Ottawa Family Court Judge J. F. McKinley informed the prime minister that, at a meeting of an organization of exconvicts over which he presided, "the release of Ryan was discussed and several plans for his rehabilitation were offered by the men." Miss Agnes MacPhail, the M.P. for Grey-Bruce, who had met Ryan while on a prison tour, raised his case on the floor of the House of Commons. One of the most dedicated of Red's interveners was Sen. Harry A. Mullins, a wealthy man and a former Conservative member of Parliament for Marquette, who had a lifelong interest in prison rehabilitation. Ryan's plight was first brought to the good senator's attention by his wife who, fourteen years earlier, had been deeply moved by the sight of Ryan in shackles at Toronto's Union Station, ready to be shipped for a lifetime in Kingston's penitentiary. "I was about to leave the old Toronto station on a trip,"

Mrs. Mullins recalled, "when I saw a man with manacles on his wrists standing a few yards away. His head was lowered and he looked beaten in spirit. I felt terribly sorry for him and even more so a few minutes later when I learned he was Norman Ryan and was preparing to spend the last of life in the penitentiary. I told my husband later my reaction." When the senator visited the penitentiary following the 1933 riots in the company of Toronto clergyman W. A. Cameron, he met Ryan and was impressed enough to argue strenuously for his parole before the Honourable Hugh Guthrie, minister of justice.

Sen. Harry Mullins was not the only prominent public figure to seek out Ryan in prison. "In the penitentiary, he was the star boarder, the most famous prisoner," a *Star* reporter observed, "when great men visited the prison, he was the prize exhibit. He was an extraordinarily good show-piece. No visitor could fail to see that he was kindly and intelligent." Canada's number one public enemy had become, in fact, Kingston Penitentiary's premier public exhibit, whose shining display attracted a host of visiting senators, magistrates, politicians, attorneys, and police officials. Among Red's most illustrious guests was the Honourable Ernest Lapointe, Guthrie's predecessor as justice minister, whose arrival at the penitentiary prompted a prisoner to comment, "It's great, isn't it, the importance of being earnest." Tim Buck, who almost lost his life during the riot of 1933, complained that when General Ormond came to the penitentiary to inquire about conditions, he sought out Red Ryan; "Then he talked with Red Ryan's closest buddies... Mickey McDonald and Sam Behan.... These were all men of the elite, men serving long sentences for crimes of violence. He didn't send for any of the Communists or those people who were most active in my classes."

Of Red's several meetings with prominent visitors, none was as fateful as his half-hour session on Wednesday, July 24, 1934, with the prime minister of Canada, the Honourable Richard Bedford Bennett. Flanked by Warden R. M. Allen, Justice Minister Guthrie, and a guard, Bennett shook Red's hand and talked with him in the corridor of the hospital ward after confessing that he had "heard quite a bit" about him. "We all chatted for a few minutes," Red later wrote, "and then the Premier took me aside and questioned me about my progress, my outlook on life in general, and plans I had formed for the future. He seemed genuinely and deeply interested and I found myself talking to him without restraint. He seemed pleased and impressed when I told him, as frankly as I knew how, just how I felt about the past and that I had made up my mind years ago to change my way of life.... Mr. Guthrie remarked that I was looking well and seemed to be in fine shape physically. Mr. Bennett at once queried: 'But how about your mental progress, Ryan, how are you getting along?'

" 'I have been trying to improve myself' I told him, 'I know you have,' he answered, 'I've been told that and I believe it.' "

After shaking hands and saying goobye, Bennett visited Red's room, which he found spotlessly clean and in good order. In a personal letter to Red's family after the visit, the prime minister wrote, "I was greatly impressed by what he said to me. ... I can only say that his demeanor, his clothes, his sleeping cot and surroundings indicated that he was being particular about everything and the books he was reading were calculated to stimulate him to renewed efforts for usefulness. The Minister charged with responsibilities in such matters is at the moment absent. When he returns, I will speak to him about the matter."

Red knew, following Bennett's visit, that the corner had been turned and that it might be only a matter of months before his parole was secured. But it could not come soon enough. Press announcements of his impending release in December, 1934, as a New Year's gift, proved premature. Several months later, when the King's jubilee remissions were announced, Red's name was not included among those chosen, an omission that moved him to write his brother: "The month which we awaited and so joyously anticipated its approach — 'The month' which should have restored to me my loved ones arrived and is almost gone. It brought not unhappiness, but a shocking disappointment and a feeling of hopeless futility ... not alone for myself, but for your faith in me." But the big break finally came in early July, 1935, following the death of Red's sister, Isabella, for years a patient in the sanitorium in Weston, when the prime minister telegramed his heartfelt condolences to the Ryan family and, in response to a request from brother Russ, released Red for a day to attend the funeral. There were no handcuffs and only a single guard — a young staff officer who had formerly served as an altar boy at Kingston's Roman Catholic cathedral — during the twelve-hour tour, which brought Red his first glimpses of freedom in twelve years. He visited with his brothers and sisters, toured the city by foot and car, took in the pink Cuban flamingos in Hyde Park, the flashing electric signs of Sunnyside, the smart new buildings of past and present benefactors: the Bank of Commerce and the *Toronto Daily Star*.

The final word came a few weeks later, on July 23 — a year less a day after Bennett's visit — when Warden Allen walked over to the hospital ward and with a smile asked Red whether he thought "it would be too wet to go out today?" When Red replied, "I'd go out in a bathing suit," the warden disclosed that the word from Ottawa had arrived and invited him to his office, where he gave him a newspaper to read, volunteered some helpful advice, and offered his view that Red would indeed never return to the penitentiary. Red then bade goodbye to his colleagues, including the segregation gang, who broke rank and rushed to the barrier to cheer him, and collected his assets: a plain brown suit; $175 in wages calculated at five cents a day under regulations recently introduced; a gold watch bequeathed to him by his father; a billfold containing various foreign denominations left over from his World War I travels; and a pullman ticket stamped October 26, 1921, the date of his arrest in Montreal, following the shooting match outside the Y.M.C.A. Red inherited as well a batch of gifts, cards, and letters, including several items from a friendly bank manager, withheld for years due to prison regulations. Among this assortment lay a letter, fourteen years old, from his young wife Elsie, professing her love. According to one account, Red had not been told of the letter and, thinking his wife had abandoned him, never bothered communicating with her or determining her whereabouts. Several years later, in 1927, he was told that she had died.

The homecoming of Toronto's repentant sinner inspired an orgy of publicity from the big dailies. Editorialists fulminated over "the scandal of Red Ryan's mails," defended his right and competence to pronounce on current penological questions and credited R. B. Bennett's character with a new and hidden side. "Mr. Bennett has not always been happy in his relations towards the unfortunate whom he has interviewed," the *Star* commented; "He has at times been brusque and arrogant. But a different side to his nature is revealed by the man who has just been released from Kingston. . . . Those who have criticized Mr. Bennett for his harshness to delegations of the unemployed will welcome this indication of a genuine kindliness of heart."

The *Star* world copyrighted an immense feature story, decorated with multi-columned photos, on Red's release and lent him prominent space in successive issues during the week of his homecoming to tell his life story. Red wrote feelingly of his childhood, the fatal drift into criminality, the successive prison experiences, the great escape and recapture, his repentance and rebirth during the agony of solitary confinement. He praised the goodness and humanity of certain individuals — R. B. Bennett, Father Kingsley, Wardens Megloughlin and Ponsford — and attacked the cruelties and deficiencies of the system: overcrowding, incompetent guards, the abuse and restrictions of mailing privileges, inadequate recreation facilities, the indiscriminate mixing of delinquent youths with hardened criminals. Above all, Red repeated the wisdom that he alone was "the true author of his past troubles" and was "retired from the banking business for good."[3]

---

3. Red wrote of his new purpose: "I regard my release as a big experiment, the success or failure of which may affect the future of hundreds of fellows, in prison and out. If, in my way of life, I can justify the faith in human nature that has given me my freedom, I will have done something to atone for the terrible mistakes of the past and make the redemption of others as unfortunate and reckless as I have been, easier and surer."

And so it seemed during the dizzy weeks following the prodigal son's homecoming — a return to Toronto the Good, which Red described as the fulfilment of a dream, a voyage of discovery into a new and kinder world. From his brother's house on Lansdowne Avenue, Red wrote the prime minister thanking him for his "very kind act and consideration" and assuring him that he would "never let down" those responsible for his freedom. And he was pleased to receive a warm reply from Bennett, expressing the earnest hope that, with Divine help, he would withstand any temptation that might beset him and succeed in settling into "a good position in the community." "You have a host of friends who wish you well and who have faith and confidence that you will succeed," Bennett wrote, "No one is more sincere in that wish than I." Red dropped in on Toronto Chief Constable Guthrie, who served as president of the Citizens Service Association for the rehabilitation of discharged inmates, and accepted an invitation to the police games at Hanlan's Point, which he attended in the company of several civic dignitaries. Senator Frank O'Connor, of Laura Secord candy store fame, spoke kind and encouraging words to Red at the police picnic, while Senator Mullins offered to send him on a speaking tour or settle him on a farm in rural Manitoba.

But there was no one whose support Red valued more than that of Father Kingsley, to whom he reported on a regular basis as stipulated in his ticket of leave. The day after his return to Toronto, Red joined Father Kingsley and His Excellency Archbishop O'Brien of Kingston at a retreat in Toronto's Saint Augustine Seminary, where a young priest, following an introduction, commented, "Ryan hardly looks like a man who ever had a gun in his hand." Red and brother Russ later joined Rev. Father Ambrose J. O'Brien at Saint Theresa's Church (the Shrine of the Little Flower on Kingston Road) where, in the cool of the evening, with a brilliant sun pouring its light through the stained-glass windows, all three knelt before the altar in brief prayer. A week later, Red returned to Kingston as guest of honor at the annual picnic and bazaar of Father Kingsley's parish held on the grounds of the Church of the Good Thief in Portsmouth. The event was attended by hundreds of local residents, many of whom — Warden Megloughlin included — sought out Ryan, shook his hand, and joined him in games of chance.

As the homecoming frenzy abated, Red settled into a routine existence. He moved into the home of his younger brother Russell on Lansdowne Avenue and accepted a position as salesman with Fawcett Motors, a Weston firm. In the evening he worked as a host, music arranger, manager, and bouncer, at the Nealan House Hotel, a lively King Street East establishment featuring singing waiters and owned by the prominent wrestling promoter, Jack Corcoran. Corcoran, who showed a warm interest in Red's rehabilitation, was unfortunately, but understandably, cool to Red's suggestion that a large sign announcing "Red Ryan is here" be placed at the front of the hotel.

Red's social and financial life, and his lively interest in prison reform matters, proceeded nicely. He was soon able to finance a roadster and a wardrobe of twelve suits. Just six months after release, he distributed with characteristic generosity over one thousand dollars in Christmas gifts, including an expensive fur coat to a young secretary. When exconvicts sought him out after release from the penitentiary, he was an easy touch and sometimes let go $100 at a time. For recreation, Red wrestled or watched matches from Jack Corcoran's box, sometimes in the company of civic dignitaries like Magistrate R. J. Browne. Major Wallace Bunton, the chief of the exprisoner's service of the Salvation Army, regularly joined him for lunch where matters affecting the welfare of exconvicts were discussed. When a new prison reform commission was contemplated in the spring of 1936, Red sought out a crown attorney in Toronto and asked to be considered for a position. He befriended Harry Anderson, the *Globe* managing editor and a fervent crusader for prison reform. When Anderson died, Red sent a wreath to his wife, who placed Red's flowers alongside the casket and, as a return gift, sent along several pages from Anderson's Bible. At the funeral service at Knox United Church, Red was prominently in view, in a front-row pew, kneeling and singing hymns throughout the solemn proceedings.

Despite his busy social life, Red never let his contact and friendship with Father Kingsley lapse. They corresponded by mail and met frequently either in Toronto, where Father occasionally visited, or in Kingston, where Red spent many warm hours supping and chatting at the parish house. Sometimes Father Kingsley invited along other old friends, like retired keeper Matt Walsh who, one day over a warm meal in the spring of 1936, noted that Red's hair, plastered as usual with Brilliantine, had oddly turned a dark brown.

Matt Walsh let his observation pass, but had he thought further about the matter, he might have recalled an earlier time, back in 1922, when Red, in the clutches of the law, was taken from Saint Vincent de Paul to Kingston Penitentiary. Among Red's meager possessions then, which Matt Walsh had had occasion to store and note, were a pair of sunglasses and a bottle of brown hair dye, the latter employed by the fugitive to cover his telltale mop. Red had never been happy with dye and complained in earlier days that it stuck too hard and was impossible to remove. But he used it then, just as he was using it now, to disguise his identity during the dark hours of robbery and flight.

Toronto's civic hero, it turned out, was leading a double life. Red Ryan performed publicly as a showcase convert; the repentant sinner scoffingly referred to by Premier Mitchell Hepburn as the pet of R. B. Bennett, who brought more joy to Good Toronto, and the angels of heaven, than the combined virtuous acts of the hordes of decent people.[4] But Red lived another life, hidden from the moral scrutiny of priests, reporters, and police; a secret life among criminal kin living forever in the shadow of the penitentiary.

It was known by Father Kingsley and others that Red fraternized on occasion with "K.P. men." But they never suspected that Red, during the months of his charade of civic virtue, consorted in a business way with the likes of Harry Checkley, a "punk" he had met in prison, who had a long record involving burglary and theft, dating as far back as 1922, when he was first arrested on an indecent assault charge in Portage La Prairie, Manitoba.[5] Nor was it known that Red had established a working partnership with Edward McMullen, once described by Warden Tucker as the most dangerous man in the Kingston Penitentiary, who was awarded a ticket of leave in May, 1934. Upon release, McMullen worked a double shift. During the day, he was known to his neighbors in east Toronto as a quiet man who minded his own business, tinkered with his car, compulsively wore a hat to cover his bald head and, depending on when asked, was employed as an oil salesman, landscaper, or wrestling promoter. At night, he robbed banks and blew safes. When Red Ryan offered his services as an undercover agent to aid the police in tracking down the killer of Edward Stonehouse, a Markham councilor shot to death — by Edward McMullen — during an attempted car theft on the night of February 29, 1936, the police little appreciated that McMullen's partner, the man who drove the getaway car and wounded Stonehouse's son during the melee, was Red Ryan himself.[6]

Ontario and Quebec were afflicted during the months of Red's settlement into the public, and publicized, role of useful citizen, by an epidemic of burglaries and robberies. Banks were held up, including the Dominion Bank of Commerce at Davenport and Laughlin in Toronto; the Ailsa Craig branch of the Bank of Commerce; the Bank of Nova Scotia in Lachute, Quebec; and the Locke and Herkimer branch of the

---

4. According to Professor Hugo McPherson, the title and theme of Morley Callaghan's, *More Joy in Heaven*, based on Ryan's story, was drawn from the fifteenth and sixteenth chapters of Luke where Jesus "assured the publicans and sinners that there will be more joy in heaven upon the repentance of one sinner than upon ninety-nine just persons who need no repentance" (Morley Callaghan, *More Joy in Heaven* [Toronto: McClelland and Stewart, 1960], Introduction).

5. Checkley spent concurrent years with Ryan in the penitentiary after being sentenced to five years for robbing the home of Lady Hughes, wife of Sir Sam Hughes.

6. According to a report of Dr. E.R. Frankish, Ontario Medical-Legal expert to Attorney General Arthur Roebuck, McMullen killed the elder Stonehouse, and Ryan wounded his son.

Bank of Commerce, Hamilton. And stores were burgled, among them the National Groceries Warehouse in Collingwood; the Scarborough Liquor Control Board; Scotts Woollen Mills and Metropolitan store in Toronto; and the Ontario Produce Marketing Company in Markham.

It was never ascertained that Red Ryan had a hand in all of these jobs. Red, after all, had a heart and in depressed times was likely inclined to spread employment opportunities and make-work projects among the needy. But there is little doubt that the Ryan gang, unknown to the police at the time, were behind several large jobs including the Lachute, Quebec bank effort, which involved the clubbing of the bank manager, a take of $3,400, and a clean getaway in a maroon Oldsmobile stolen on April 5, in Toronto and outfitted as usual with stolen and altered plates.

It was, indeed, the same car, with changed plates, which carried Red and Harry Checkley to Sarnia, Ontario, in the early afternoon of May 25, following a hurried lunch at Russ Ryan's Lansdowne Avenue house. Their destination was the Sarnia liquor store — a bare block from the local police station — which, Red surmised, was ready for a hefty take on account of long-weekend sales. Dressed in railway overalls, the bandits parked their car on a sidestreet a block away, cut through a back lane, and, at five minutes before 6:00 P.M. — closing time — slipped through the entrance door, which they locked before outfitting themselves with railway caps, handkerchiefs, masks, and dark goggles.

Red and Chuck, as his partner was known, stationed themselves at the bottom of the stairwell leading up to the main floor of the store and waited for the crowd upstairs to thin out through a separate exit. But they were forced into action early — at two or three minutes to six — when their presence was discovered by a customer, a Mr. Austin Glass, who, short of change, had peeked down the entrance stairway in the hope of spotting a helpful friend.

Checkley arrived at the sales floor first and, with a gun in each hand, rushed to the middle of the floor, shouted to the customers — there were still over twenty in the store — to stick up their hands, turn their backs, and face the walls. Red then vaulted the counter, trained his guns, a .45-caliber Colt automatic and a .38-caliber Iver Johnson revolver, on the manager and staff, and proceeded to empty the till.

Unfortunately for Red and Chuck, the scene did not go unnoticed by a Mr. Geoffrey Garvey, an oil company employee who arrived at the store at the very moment the bandits went into play. Finding the front entrance locked, and moved by the gloomy prospect of a dry weekend, Mr. Garvey had decided to duck into the store through the exit door and stairway, only to notice as he arrived, the entire gallery of customers in the sales area of the main floor, standing with their arms raised. The bandits, unlike several customers, did not see Mr. Garvey, who disappeared across the street to inform a local cab driver waiting at a stand. A quick phone call to the police station a block away brought, in a matter of seconds, four policemen to the scene in a cruiser car. While Constable William Simpkins guarded the locked entrance door, his three colleagues, Sergeant George Smith, Detective Frank McGirr, and Constable John Lewis, rushed with guns drawn through the exit and up the stairs towards the sales area.

Red was ready to leave, with a miserable total take of $394.26, when he heard the crash of the door closing downstairs and the rush of footsteps up the stairway. Constable Lewis, who led the invasion, reached the floor first and was only four feet away when Red fired four shots into his chest. Lewis collapsed, mortally wounded, at the top of the stairway but close behind rushed his two colleagues, their guns firing. Red traded shots and took a bullet in the ankle before retreating with Checkley across the store and down the stairway leading to the locked entrance. Checkley was halfway down when the officers, firing discreetly from around the corner, scored with a fatal shot, causing him to drop his gun and shout that he was finished. Red, in the meanwhile, fumbled with the lock on the door below and emptied the gun in his free hand with a volley of shots up the stairway. But he was exposed and trapped below, and took bullets in the arm and neck before throwing his guns on the landing above and collapsing in a pool of blood alongside his dead partner.

Red Ryan, the volatile Irishman who rarely missed a chance to shake a hand, or preach, or rob a bank, died within two hours, after removal to a hospital by ambulance, through a crowd of excited spectators who had gathered outside the liquor store during the violent exchange and cheered the news of the bandits' death. When the police discovered that the big man with the dark-brown hair carried a license in his wallet belonging to a Norman J. Ryan, the word hit the headlines of the front pages of the big dailies from Sarnia, Ontario, to Victoria, British Columbia. The next day, in a Sarnia funeral parlor, where the two bandits lay on separate divans, under gold coverlets turned back to show their wounds, an estimated six thousand curious people filed by the corpses for a look and a frown.

Red's final homecoming, in a casket, drew no such crowd. It was, indeed, ignored by the very masses and beautiful people who had cheered his miraculous conversion only ten months earlier. When the body, in a gray pine box, arrived near midnight the next day at Toronto's Union Station accompanied by Russ Ryan, only Jack Corcoran and the mortician, a Mr. Charles Connors of Avenue Road, were there to greet it. The sole mourners at the burial, at Mount Hope cemetery, were Red's brother, Russ, and a sister-in-law. By order of Archbishop James J.

McGuigan, Red Ryan was denied the last rites of the Roman Catholic church and was interred on unconsecrated ground.

No mass, or committal service, or priestly presence graced the final interment of Red Ryan, whose seamy demise inspired Mr. Justice Henderson to predict, in the Court of Appeal at Osgoode Hall, that there would be "no more heroes among criminals in Canada for some time." In the weeks following the Sarnia denouement, Red's fate was mused upon by editorialists, his character dissected by psychologists, and his memory cursed by a legion of former admirers, including the embittered Father Kingsley, who felt that Red had recklessly cast aside "all the leniency of the law, the generosity of society, the forbearance of the public." While reformers and law-and-order people debated the liberalization of the parole system — which Red's performance set back a few years, or decades — politicians like George Drew likened the dead outlaw with Baby Face Nelson and John Dillinger and located the source of the problem in the other fellow's federal, provincial, or partisan backyard. But in the storm of words following Red's demise, there were few commentators, if any, who could summon a kind word for the dead man, or, at least, credit him with honoring his commitment never to return to the Kingston Penitentiary.[7]

---

7. Edward McMullen, who had fled to Vancouver before the Sarnia robbery, also never made it back. Several days after Red's death McMullen was intercepted at the Blaine crossing into the United States and accidentally shot himself during a fight following his murder of a border guard.

4
HOT CARGO

It was no pretty sight. The throat had been slashed from ear to ear, by a hand razor presumably, which lay at the dead man's side. Nearby was an empty whisky flask. The ankles of the deceased — Mr. Harnam Singh of Vancouver, British Columbia — were bound together with dirty white muslin, unraveled from the victim's own turban.

The dead man was a new Canadian, a Sikh, from the Punjab region of India who, with several thousand of his kin, sought in British Columbia the good and quiet life as outlined in C.P.R. travel brochures and like documents. Instead, he landed in a cauldron of hatred and feuding so bitter that a score of lives were lost before emotions subsided in the middle years of World War I.

The source of the violence and vendetta lay in the failed hopes of Hindus — as they were sometimes known — settled, or wishing to settle, in a society bent on keeping its racial coloration a pure and snowy white. As loyal British subjects, the migratory Indians believed they were entitled to locate freely anywhere within the Empire, including the rich, vast, and vacant land of British Columbia. White Canada, however, disputed the claim and, in doing so, employed methods and erected barriers that invited a wave of agitation and outlawry reaching the entire way from Kitsilano, British Columbia to Amritsar, India.

The Indian migration to British Columbia began around the turn of the century in response to land pressures in the central and western Punjab; an incurable wanderlust among émigré colonists in east and southeast Asia; and, oddly enough, encouragements from Canada. An independent, martial people, who congregated primarily in the Punjab in the mid-nineteenth century, the Sikhs made peace with the British following the decline of Ranjit Singh's Empire and the conclusion of the Anglo-Sikh wars of 1846-49. Attracted to the "canal colonies" fostered by the British in the wheat growing region of the western Punjab, the peasants soon found themselves crowded out by moneylenders, speculators, and hungry émigrés from the south, where several failed monsoons and droughts had driven numerous farmers from the land. The inability of the canal colonies to absorb the surplus labor forced a migration eastward to Bengal and the British possessions beyond, in Burma, Hong Kong, and the coast of China. By the century's end, communities could be found in Singapore, Thailand, the Netherlands, East Indies, Philippines, and the coast of North America.

The diffusion eastward little resembled other migrations from India, to the Caribbean and East Africa, where, in countries like Mauritius, British Guiana, and Trinidad, indentured labor from eastern India — mainly Tamils and Telugus — had been imported to work on plantations deserted by freed slaves. The migratory Sikhs were, relatively speaking, substantial peasants who had rendered useful service to the British Imperial machine. Following their subjugation by the British, the Sikhs had become loyal subjects of the Crown, enlisting as Imperial minions, and joining the ruling power in quelling the mutiny of 1857. Thereafter, they provided an important recruiting ground for the army and, in the British Asian concessions in places like Upper Burma, Hankow, Hong Kong, and Shanghai, served faithfully as soldiers, watchmen, bank guards, and police.

The Indians who arrived via Hong Kong and Yokohama in the C.P.R. steamers the *Monteagle* and *Tartar* at the British Columbia ports of Vancouver and Victoria in the early years of the century were, except for a minority of Hindus and Muslims, Sikhs from India or the British possessions in East Asia; men with peasant, military, and police backgrounds, some on leave or retired from service, touchy on matters of honor, physically strong and disciplined, and fully cognizant of the Imperial dues paid. Some heard of opportunities in British Columbia from the British during the Boxer Rebellion or from Chinese in the port cities who preceded them to the New World. Others, who attended the Silver Jubilee celebration in London in 1897, marveled at the vast and unspoiled wilderness they passed through on their return and resolved, on returning to Asia, to move to the new land. Nor were Canadian employers and steamship companies, anxious for profits and willing hands in a labor-scarce province with bright prospects of industrial expansion, remiss in advertising the possibilities of relocation. Railway contractors and lumber magnates encouraged their entry, in consort with labor contractors like Gillanders, Arbuthnot and Co., and the C.P.R., whose steamship service across the north Pacific sought a full supply of human cargo. Soon after arriving in North America, the Sikhs themselves joined the celebration and, after sampling wages and tasting property ownership seldom known before, encouraged their waiting kin with rosy letters outlining the bright prospects of the New World.

The kin came. In 1904, a mere 258 were recorded as resident in the province. Two years later, however, a further 1,250 embarked, followed by 4,700 in the next two years. The immigrants were mostly young men of working age, who sought employment as lumber-mill hands, on railway construction, or as farm laborers. They congregated mainly in Vancouver, although some resided on the Island or settled in the interior. A strong, sturdy, and conditioned people, the Sikhs were willing workers, prepared to settle for wages one-half or one-third of those received by white employees in similar occupations.

The white workers did not value the competition of a group who soon shared with the other Orientals who had preceded them, the Chinese and Japanese, a virtual pariah status. By the time the Sikhs arrived, white British Columbia had arrived at a clear and firm consensus about the undesirability of Orientals who, it was alleged, resisted unionization, undercut white wages, sometimes served as strike-breakers, and, in rising numbers, threatened to inundate and submerge a precarious, weakly-formed white culture. Stereotypes formed which expressed and legitimated white hostilities. Present as early as the gold rush, the Chinese were viewed as filthy, diseased, clannish, unassimilable, and bent on

"Hindus" camping on the sidewalk in Vancouver, November, 1905. City Archives, Vancouver

undermining both the purity of the white race and the wage levels of decent white workers. The Japanese suffered under equally onerous, though different, stereotypes. Beginning in the 1870s, a series of laws were passed by the provincial legislature barring the entry of Orientals and curtailing the rights of those already in. Head, poll, and entry taxes were introduced and then increased; property ownership restrictions imposed; and the right of suffrage denied. Daily prejudice and discrimination were supplemented in stressful times by rioting such as the outbreak in Victoria and Vancouver in 1886, when white working men rampaged against the local Chinese. Exclusion Leagues and Workingmen's Associations met, resolved, demonstrated, and petitioned politicians, who competed with one another in verbally flogging the newcomers and legislating restrictions.

The Sikhs were welcomed in similar ways, by a charter group uncertain of its own identity and tenancy of a rich and inviting resource empire. Tall, dark, bearded, and turbaned, the Sikhs were so "conspicuous," a pair of Indian writers observed, that they were visible from "a mile away." Though many flaunted their war medals, disparagingly referred to in the local press as "tin pot decorations," few whites were prepared to accept them as Empire equals. From the day of their entry, they were labeled by a hostile press, the politicians, and an army of exclusionists as unclean, disease-ridden, polygamous, caste-riven, inordinately fecund, unadaptable, and unassimilable. "The transfer of any people from a tropical climate to a northern one," declared W. B. Scott, federal superintendent of immigration, "must of necessity result in much physical suffering and danger to health, not only on account of non-acclimatization, but also on account of ignorance in the matter of housing, food and clothing."[1] A *Vancouver Sun* journalist found them, in 1914, "pitiable." "They have left their native land," wrote Albert Foote, "with its humid, terrific eternal heat and landing in our cool climate, shivered continuously. If you have ever seen one of those nasty, hairless Mexican dogs, trembling and shaking up here on a cold, raw day, you can get what I mean." W. L. MacKenzie King, who reported on Indian immigration into Canada in 1908, thought, "the native of India is not a person suited to this country,"[2] a view shared by a *Sun* editorial writer,

---

1. Scott's views were hardly shared by a Dr. S.H. Lawson, a physician attending the C.P.R. steamer *Monteagle* at Hong Kong, where he examined the steerage passengers and concluded: "They were 100 percent cleaner in their habits and freer from disease than the European steerage passengers I had come in contact with. My more recent impressions as a surgeon in mining camps among thousands of white men, where immorality is rife, has increased my respect for the Sikhs."

2. The *Saturday Sunset* wrote on the same subject: "We don't care whether the Hindu is 'born under the flag' or not. If he could peroxide himself white, it would not make any difference."

who wrote in November, 1913, of the Orientals as "vicious, untruthful and seditious people, whom we could not assimilate if we desired to, but who we should not wish to if one could, as they would destroy the Canadian type mentally and physically."

As public trustees and designated keepers of the purity of the Canadian type, the politicians acted accordingly. Any reticence that may have existed about the need to legislate a rigid exclusion disappeared with the riots of 1907, when the local Chinese and Japanese were besieged in their ghettos by a crazed force of white purists. Although the Sikhs, hidden in their Gurdwaras[3] some distance from the field of action, escaped the violence, the sudden arrival in July, 1907, of 1,500 of their number along with a shipment of 7,000 Japanese, had contributed substantially to the sudden outbreak. The riots inflamed opinion against all Orientals and encouraged exclusionists like Vancouver Mayor Buscombe who, taking a cue from the Vancouver and Victoria labor councils, as well as his own city council, prevailed on the C.P.R. officials in August, 1906, to detain and eventually divert to Victoria a shipload of East Indians on the grounds they were likely to become public charges.

The mayor was not alone in his views. A host of civic and provincial politicians petitioned the federal Liberal government of Sir Wilfrid Laurier, who, in a letter to the viceroy of India, Lord Minto, wrote, "strange to say, the Hindus . . . are looked on by our people in British Columbia with still more disfavour than the Chinese. They seem to be less adaptable to our ways and manners than all the other Oriental races that came to us." Under the existing immigration regulations, Laurier's minions in the Immigration Department were free to use any of several administrative rules and procedures to exclude immigrants, including a section of the Immigration Act of 1906 that authorized officials to bar would-be immigrants or deport those already landed — within two years of their arrival — thought to be paupers, beggars, vagrants, destitutes, or "likely to become a public charge." When this failed, the officials could fall back on medical examinations at ports of entry to disclose any of several debilitating or excommunicable diseases, ranging from trachoma to conjunctivitis. As local opinion heated, however, the officials looked for something more; a means of preventing or discouraging "Hindus" from even attempting a run at Canada's golden western shores.

With this need in mind, the federal government resorted to the twin methods of diplomacy and legislation. A young star in the Department of Labour who at a tender age had earned a considerable reputation on

3. The Sikh temple was called Gurdwara or "the Gateway of the Guru." The central object of worship in the temple was the Holy Book — the *Granth Sahib.*

labor matters, was dispatched on a tour to Britain and India, where colonial officials were pressed to join an exclusionist crusade. The first stop of W. L. MacKenzie King's voyage was Vancouver, where he sampled local opinion, observed conditions first hand, and mournfully concluded that British Columbia's damp climate and environment was likely to make the Indian situation "unhappy and unhopeful": "The native of India . . . is not a person suited to this country . . . accustomed as many of them are to the conditions of a tropical climate, and possessing manners and customs so unlike those of our own people, their mobility, their inability to readily adapt themselves to surroundings entirely different could not do other than entail an amount of privation and suffering which render a discontinuance of such immigration most desirable in the interests of the Indians themselves." King went on to London where the colonial secretary, Lord Elgin, and John Morley, the secretary of state, were impressed with Canada's autonomous right to decide who may, or may not, enter the Dominion, and King urged them to implement a restrictive quota and permit system. The tour ended in Calcutta, where King put the case before Viceroy Lord Minto for a permit and quota system and reminded Minto of India's Immigration Act of 1883, originally passed to safeguard the interests of indentured servants, which barred emigration from India to countries, like Canada, that had not instituted protective legislation. Minto agreed to sponsor a campaign informing prospective emigrants about "poor employment conditions" in Canada and to order shipping companies to desist from advertising travel facilities. Any restrictive measures enacted or contemplated by Canada, the viceroy promised, would be given full publicity.

Restrictive legislation preceded and followed King's tour. In keeping with the emergent doctrine of Dominion autonomy, which guaranteed the rights of new nations of European blood within the Empire "to decide for themselves whom in each case they will admit as citizens of their respective Dominions," the Laurier government slipped through an order-in-council in January, 1908, granting the minister of the interior the right to prohibit immigrants from landing in Canada "unless they came from the country of their birth or citizenship by a continuous journey, and on through tickets purchased before leaving the country of their birth or citizenship." In June, a second order passed, requiring any Asians entering Canada from a country without special treaty rights to possess a minimum of $200.

Both measures were directed specifically at Indian immigrants without naming them as a group. The $200 entry-tax rule hardly applied to Japanese immigration, already regulated by existing treaties and "special arrangements" such as the Lemieux Agreement, which restricted, by mutual agreement between the Japanese, Imperial, and Canadian authorities, the ingress of Japanese immigrants to 400 per year. Although the "continuous journey" ruling made no mention of "Hindus" or other national groups, its intent, according to the exclusionist M.P. H. H. Stevens, a member of Parliament for Vancouver, was to "keep the Hindus out and at the same time render the Government immune from attack on the grounds that they were passing regulations against the interest of the Hindus who are British subjects." Japanese or Chinese could travel directly from their home ports to Canada on ships that plied the route directly, without impinging on the continuous-journey provision. Indians, however, were effectively barred since no direct steamship line connected their home country with Canada. Travelers from India had to be transshipped out of Yokohama, Hong Kong, or other ports.

Laurier's new orders did the job. When the C.P.R. steamship *Monteagle* pulled into Vancouver's harbor in March, 1908, the bulk of its Indian passengers were turned back since, in boarding in Hong Kong, they had not come by direct passage from India, their place of birth or citizenship. Another group, who boarded ship at Calcutta, suffered a like fate because they could not prove that they were the men who had purchased the tickets at Calcutta and not imposters. In 1909-10, a mere sixteen Indians were admitted into the country. By 1911, British Columbia's Indian community numbered under twenty-five hundred, less than half of what it had been in the peak year of 1908. The new restrictions not merely halted immigration; they invited the departure of those already landed back to India, the China ports, or south to the United States, where the Sikh communities of farmhands, lumbermen, and laborers in Washington, Oregon, and, primarily, California, had grown, by 1910, to six thousand.

The remnants in British Columbia, in the meanwhile, survived in a virtual state of siege, social ostracism, and administrative harrassment. Not content with halting immigration, the minister of the interior looked for ways of transporting the existing remnants elsewhere. After considering British Panama, Fiji, and the Philippines, the Honourable Frank Oliver and his private secretary, Mr. J. B. Harkin, settled on the British Honduras, already well served by indentured labor, as a suitable and humane locale. Harkin sought and obtained the approval of the Honduras governor before inviting a pair of representatives from the Vancouver Indian community to join himself and an immigration department official, a Mr. W. C. Hopkinson, on an exploratory tour of the Central American country. The Indians, it appeared, were not impressed with their designated malarial home and, at a public meeting at which Hopkinson and Harkin hoped the scheme would be sold, reported unfavorably on what they had seen and denounced the venture. The scheme subsequently died.

But the harrassment continued. American Sikhs, formerly residents of British Columbia, who wished to return there to attend to matters affecting property they had purchased before departure, were allowed in, on temporary passes, only after a long fight. More galling was the treatment accorded the wives and children of residents, who were prevented from joining their sojourning fathers and husbands. In 1912, the wives of Balwant Singh and Bhag Singh, a former trooper of the British India Cavalry, policeman in Hangkow, and secretary of the Sikh Trust Company, who served as president of the Vancouver Gurdwara, were allowed to enter only after a six-month agitation, a spate of hearings, and "as an act of Grace without establishing precedent." In two subsequent years, only five wives, a mother, and thirteen children, were allowed in.

All of this did make for a quiescent Indian citizenry. Shunned like the pox, the Sikhs pulled together, organized, practiced self-help, and pressed the authorities to improve conditions. Soon after the arrival of the first immigrants, branches of the Khalsa Diwan Society, or Free Divine Communion, appeared in Vancouver, Victoria, Abbotsford, New Westminster, Fraser Mills, and Ocean Falls, and took on religious, welfare, educational, and philanthropic functions. In 1908, Sikhs formed a colonization company on a cooperative basis, bought two hundred acres near Vancouver, and put up houses. Temples built and owned by the Khalsa Diwan Societies in Vancouver and Victoria served as places of worship, cultural centers, distribution centers of aid to indigent Indians, and political forums where, before and after prayers, immigration issues and other pressing matters were debated. A vernacular tabloid press emerged, along with a moderate leadership committed to influence opinion in the larger community, enlist the aid of Christian sympathizers, and petition the highest authorities in London and Calcutta for redress of grievances. At the 1911 Imperial Conference, a delegation of local Indians, assisted by the Reverend L. B. Hall of the Hindu Friends Society of Victoria, British Columbia, petitioned the delegates in the name of "sober, industrious, reliable, law-abiding" Sikh people, to ensure that "no injustice shall minimize the rights or privileges of . . . citizenship . . . whether the holder is black or white." Later in the year, three prominent leaders of the British Columbia community, Sundar Singh, Teja Singh, and Raja Singh, who represented the Khalsa Diwan Society and United India League — an umbrella organization of Sikhs, Hindus, and Muslims — reminded the new Conservative minister of the interior, the Honourable Robert Rogers, and Mr. H. H. Stevens, M.P., of the Sikhs' "fidelity and heroic loyalty to the Empire" and "inherent right to travel and reside in any part of the Empire." In 1913, a trio of new emissaries — Messrs. Balwant Singh, Nand Singh Sihra, and Narain Singh — visited London and India, where the new viceroy — Lord Hardinge — was importuned to redress grievances including the refusal to admit the wives and children of Indians landed in Canada. The delegates met with representatives of the Indian National Congress and addressed mass public meetings in the big cities, where immigration restrictions, particularly to Canada and North America, had become a live issue among nationalists of varying persuasions. In the summer of 1913, Lieutenant Governor Michael O'Dwyer wrote, "Three Sikh delegates came from Canada to the Punjab. ... They held meetings throughout the province, some of which were attended by men of undoubted loyalty. But after a time the tone of these meetings changed. Instead of reasonable criticism of the immigration laws, the speeches became menacing and inflammatory."

The new deputizers were symptomatic of changes in the leadership and strategy of the community in British Columbia. Men like Dr. Sundar Singh and Kartar Singh Akali, who, for years, edited the *Theosophical News* in Toronto, were moderate, vainly seeking respectability in a society that, in matters of immigration, preferred sheepskin coats to muslin turbans. They spoke gently to organizations like the Empire Club, focused primarily on immigration issues, memorialized elites — kings, viceroys, governors, and prime ministers — and, through organizations like the Canada India League and tabloid journals like *The Aryan*, edited by Sundar Singh, appealed to the humane sentiments of sympathetic Christians.[4] As the immigration question heated, however, these gentlemen found themselves pressed and eventually displaced by a new, more radical leadership, exemplified in the community's early years by men like Taraknath Das, a young Bengali briefly employed as a translator by the United States immigration authorities in Vancouver. Das advertised the plight of the émigré colonies and demanded a self-governing India in his tabloid the *Free Hindustan*, published in 1907, which proclaimed "Resistance To Tyranny is Obedience to God," and exhorted the Indian masses to press their leaders to halt the exclusion of laborers from Canada. He opened a school at Millside, lectured on subjects ranging from local discrimination to unrest in India, and translated and shipped to India and elsewhere bundles of radical literature.

Das's Canadian residency was short. On the urgings of British

---

4. Dr. Sundar S. Singh headed the Canada India League and founded *The Aryan* and later the *Samsar*, which was taken over by radicals. Kartar Singh Akali edited the *Theosophical News* from Toronto.

intelligence, he was returned to the United States, where the *Free Hindustan* served as the mouthpiece of an organization known as the Indian Independence League, which Das helped to found. The *Free Hindustan* promoted the cause of Sikh settlers in the lumbering and farm regions of Washington, Oregon, and California — mainly in the San Joaquin, Sacramento, and Imperial Valleys — threatened by the agitation of nativist politicians assembled in organizations like the Asiatic Exclusion League and Native Sons of the Golden West, which were devoted to stemming Turbaned Tides, Raghead Invasions, and Yellow Perils. The nativists soon had their way, and severe immigration restrictions were imposed in a country that had earlier served as a haven for émigré nationalists, some from Brahmin and Bengali elite groups, forced abroad from India by increased police pressure.

The shining star of the American-based agitators was a Bengali student and lecturer, Har Dayal, who assisted, in 1913, in the formation of the Hindu Association of America — an organization that drew strong support from Canada's disaffected Sikhs. A Delhi Kayastha, Har Dayal studied at Saint Patrick's, the University of the Punjab, and Oxford University before embarking on an itinerant radical career that took him to Parish, back to India, and finally to California, where he lectured briefly at Stanford in philosophy. The goal of Har Dayal's Hindu Association of the Pacific Coast, formed in Astoria, Washington at a meeting of Canadian and American delegates and headquartered in San Francisco, was, quite simply, revolution in India; the overthrow of the British Raj by armed force and the establishment in its place of a self-governing democratic republic. In pursuit of this end, Indians at home and abroad, in India and throughout Asia and North America, were treated to a lively campaign of propaganda. Lecturers were dispatched, and pamphlets were assembled and distributed. A weekly newspaper appeared called *Ghadar*, or *Mutiny*, in honor of the failed rising of 1857. Translated into Urdu, Gurmukhi, and English, *Ghadar* spoke hopefully of the German threat to British power; exposed British crimes in India; glorified, in biographical sketches, past patriots and contemporary freedom fighters; and, in regular excursions into the realm of culture, wrote of "the great height attained by the Indians in the past in various branches of art, science and letters, in order to give lie direct to British propaganda . . . which had been hitherto going unchecked, that the Indians occupied a very low rung in the ladder of civilization." Liberally spiced with stirring poetry professing love of country and exhorting mutiny, the *Ghadar* was read and recited at meetings in Gurdwaras as far afield as Stockton, California; Singapore; and Shanghai, China.

The fiery message of the *Ghadar* did not go unheard in the Sikh

97

temples in Victoria and Vancouver, where the followers of the divine message of Sri Guru Nanak congregated to kneel, pray, recite from the sacred *Granth Sahib*, and, alas, quarrel over political strategies. Like their home society, the Indian émigré community and organizations were afflicted by nagging social differences, factionalism, and a litigious spirit, which hampered united action. "Very common is court litigation among the Hindustanis," a student of the Pacific Coast workers reported; "from Imperial Valley to British Columbia this complaint has repeatedly been made by the Americans and Canadians. In fact, it is the most serious defect among them. They quarrel among themselves and often go to court for decisions. Even the major crimes such as murder result from personal petty quarrels."[5] Social differences, between the Sikhs, many of whom were illiterate laborers, and the educated Bengalis, were a common cause of tension. "The Sikhs were looked down upon by the Hindus," a pair of Sikh writers observed, "and expected to do what they were told. Hindus treated the Sikhs with the contempt a lawyer treats his rustic client from whom he draws money. The conflict often lead to tragic results."[6] Among the Sikhs themselves, "one casteless fraternity" that, centuries ago, had heeded the ordinance of the Guru Gobind Singh to adopt the common martial name of Singh,[7] political disputes abounded between loyalists, some informers pledged to serve King and country, and radical activists soured by discriminatory immigration politics and drawn to the warming light of the *Ghadar*.

The Ghadarites and their sympathizers did not escape the notice of both British and Canadian authorities, who, from the earliest days of the immigration agitation, had closely monitored and controlled the comings

5.   The author located the source of the problem in the absence of family life among many immigrants, the prevalence of partnership as a form of business, and social conditions forcing immigrants "to live too much among themselves." In an editorial dated January 6, 1914, the *New Westminster News* fulminated: "Nothing tickles the latter [the Hindu] so much as an opportunity to project his smelly carcass into the limelight where he will be the centre of public gaze . . . the result is that the courts of British Columbia today are cloggged with cases, which have no right to be there and out of which it is eternally impossible for any person to extract justice . . . a learned judge recently characterized Hindu witnesses as the worst perjurers that came before him."

6.   An Indian nationalist who had been resident in the United States for years found the Bengali revolutionaries parochial and "absolutely unprincipled both in the conduct of their campaign and in the obtaining and spending of funds. Their patriotism was tainted by considerations of gain or profit." Sikh revolutionaries, on the other hand, proved "pure, more unselfish and disciplined" and "always lived a life of self-abnegation putting themselves invariably in positions of danger."

7.   Sikh men carry the name Singh or "lion." The women include the name Kaur. Not all Singhs and Kaurs, however, are Sikhs. The name Singh and its female counterpart were common amongst the Hindu martial classes, like the Rajputs and Gurkhas, long before Guru Gobind Singh made them obligatory for all his followers.

and goings of itinerant agitators. The British had a special interest in the Sikhs, who, though a tiny element of the population of India, were "both valued and feared by their . . . rulers." "The seriousness of the question, as regards the British Empire in India," the Indian office noted in 1915, "is that the people of the Punjab, the chief recruiting ground for the Indian Army, are the class of Indians practically affected, and the grievances of the Sikhs as regards Canada have been skillfully utilized by agitators to excite discontent in the Punjab. . . . The classes of Indians who go to South Africa are of no military importance; but the Sikhs, ever since the Indian Mutiny, have been a most important element, and the attempts of agitators to tamper with them have been closely connected with immigration grievances." Soon after his propagandizing began, Taraknath Das was throttled by a government committed, as early as 1908, to spiking "the guns of the Indian agitators in Canada." At the instigation of Canadian officials, who protested to Washington about Das's attacks on "British prestige," he was dismissed in April, 1908, from his job as a translator with the American immigration service in Vancouver. Canadian officials subsequently seized a consignment of his *Free Hindustan*, refused to transmit other issues through the mails, and leaked information on the activities of his Millside School to the Vancouver press, whose negative publicity caused its early closure.

The key monitoring agent of Mr. Das's activities and of the "alleged Hindu conspiracy" in British Columbia, was a Mr. William Charles Hopkinson, an employee of the Criminal Intelligence Department in India who was recruited in 1907 as a special agent by the immigration branch of Canada's Department of the Interior. Born in Delhi around 1880, Hopkinson learned a variety of Punjabi dialects during his early childhood. Following the death in action of his father, an officer who had escorted British Ambassador Sir Louis Cavagnieri to Kabul in 1878, Hopkinson joined the Indian Volunteer Rifles at an early age and served as an inspector of police in Calcutta before transferring to Vancouver on a leave of absence.[8] Here he married; fathered two children; bought a modest home on Barclay Street; attended Gurdwara meetings disguised

---

8.   Indian leaders like G.S. Kumar maintained that Hopkinson did "not understand Punjabi language of the Punjabis forming 95 percent of the Indian population." They insisted that Hopkinson "intentionally or unintentionally rendered misinterpretation of deposition in courts and immigration department and thus justice being miscarried and many of the Hindus, Sikhs and Mohammedans being victimized." The Indians demanded someone "well up both in mother tongue and English be substituted in his place." Both the *Daily Province* and *Daily World* agreed with Hopkinson's own resume, completed for the Department of the Interior, that he was born in Hull, Yorkshire, England. Hugh Johnston, however, in his *The Voyage of the Komagata Maru*, (Delhi: Oxford University Press, 1979), pp. 1, 142, cites Indian office baptismal records in suppport of his claim that Hopkinson was born in Delhi. A further question remains as to whether Hopkinson was Anglo-Indian, born of a British father and Indian mother.

— according to several accounts — in a false black beard, moustache, turban, dark glasses, and worn clothes; served in the 6th Regiment and "C" Company; and delivered lectures to the Vancouver police force on the Bertillon system of thumbprint measurement and identification — an expertise that stood him well in immigration matters.

A shrewd and cautious man, sensitive — according to H. H. Stevens — to the "subtleties of the Oriental mind," Hopkinson faithfully served his masters in both the Indian office and Ottawa. Following the confiscation of Mr. Das's paper, the closure of the school, and the transfer of Das's person and activities south of the border, all of which Hopkinson arranged, the British Honduras relocation scheme briefly occupied his attentions. According to one of the pair of Indian delegates who accompanied Messrs. Harkin and Hopkinson to the Central American republic, Hopkinson offered him a bribe of $3,000 and favorable consideration of an immigration application for his family, for a favorable report. Instead, the gentleman exposed and denounced Hopkinson's offer at a public meeting, which rejected the scheme and heard, in reply, Hopkinson's own claim that he had himself been subject to unwarranted pressures from opponents of the scheme within the local Indian community.

The death of the Honduras scheme hardly ended the activities of W. C. Hopkinson, who, in subsequent years, employed every means at his disposal — fair and foul — to smell out, disclose, and expel radicals, agitators, impersonators, and other guests Her Majesty's immigration minions deemed to be undesirable. He reported regularly to his superiors on organizations like G. S. Kumar's Hindustani Association of British Columbia, recruited informers within the Indian community, and collected and relayed to the authorities samples of incendiary literature and bomb manuals circulating in the mails. Hopkinson traveled south to Seattle, Berkeley, San Francisco, Astoria, and other places to keep tabs on student radicals; hired informants; liaised with the British consuls in American cities; consulted and advised the Americans on immigration restrictions; and regulated the flow of political itinerants across the border. According to his Canadian enemies, he supplemented his income with side money taken from prospective immigrants seeking favorable consideration of their applications.[9]

Hopkinson did not perform alone. Aiding him within the Indian community was a coterie of informers who, for a valuable consideration, would disclose to the authorities the "seditious" activities of their

---

9. Hopkinson wore many hats. In addition to his employment by the Indian authorites, by the immigration branch of the Department of the Interior, and his swearing in as a Dominion police constable, he received a stipend from the United States immigration service.

colleagues. The tallest of the "immigration dogs," as they were known to their opponents, was an athletic and fearless former signaler in the 20th Punjabi Regiment, Bela Singh, of the village Jaina in the district of Hashiarpur, "an exceptionally fine specimen of a Sikh, tall and straight and with military bearing . . . considered to be the handsomest Sikh in Canada." Bela immigrated to Victoria on the *Empress of Russia* in 1906, moved to Vancouver four years later, bought and sold real estate, and supplemented his income by performing "special services" for the Immigration Department. He recruited friends like Baboo Singh and Ganga Ram as informers; attended and reported on meetings at the Second Avenue temple, Dominion Hall, and other places where immigration matters were hotly debated and *Ghadar* poetry was recited; and assisted Hopkinson as court witness and translator.

Bela played a key role in the celebrated case of Natha Singh, who turned out to be the priest Bhagwan Singh Gyani, a popular orator, agitator, and *Ghadar* supporter in the Gurdwaras of the China coast. Following hearings before a special board of inquiry of the Immigration Department, at which Bela testified to Natha Singh's true identity, a deportation order was issued. Aided by sympathetic shore colleagues, the priest applied for a writ of habeas corpus and won in the Court of Appeal. But Superintendent Malcolm Reid of the Immigration Department did not see fit to deliver up his man. With the habeas corpus application pending, Bhagwan was forcibly removed by the immigration officials and their henchmen and placed on an outgoing ship to Hong Kong.

Bela's role in Bhagwan's deportation hardly excited the admiration of the friends of the *Ghadar*, who, in the months preceding the outbreak of the First World War, launched a campaign of vilification and intimidation against the immigration authorities and their minions. The agitators were given hope and encouragement by the affair of the *Panama Maru*, a Japanese ship that landed in Vancouver harbor in October, 1913, carrying a contingent of Indians. While several were admitted, a large number were detained, brought before a board of inquiry, and ordered deported. Supported and financed by their landed kin, the deportees took the case to the Court of Appeal and eventually were ordered released, on a writ of habeas corpus, by the Liberal Chief Justice Gordon Hunter. In a momentous decision, Hunter ruled that the orders-in-council P.C. 920 and 926, 1910, containing the continuous-journey and $200 entrance requirement, were ultra vires and not in conformity with the intent of the section of the Immigration Act (1910) under which they purported to be made.

The *Panama Maru* decision emboldened the immigration activists and placed the lives and livelihood of Bela Singh and his colleagues in jeopardy. "A person who is mercenary or looking for fame can never be loyal," the *Ghadar* admonished its readership. "In your way there will be some traitors who will do their best to hinder you . . . they are the wolves of the English Government. Arrangements should be made to fix these men . . . these traitorous secret service police for the sake of a few rupees are cutting the roots of the nation." The tone of the *Sansai*, a paper issued from Vancouver, became so strident during the Bhagwan Singh and *Panama Maru* affairs, that immigration agent Malcolm R. J. Reid, who sent along copies to H. H. Stevens for his perusal, concluded that it "seems to have reached a seditionary aspect." A similar boldness and excitement was evident at Gurdwara meetings, which, Reid was convinced, were part of a campaign, "to stir up an agitation to wipe me off the map." During the *Panama Maru* affair, damage suits totaling $2,000 for false arrest, imprisonment, and malicious prosecution were launched against Reid by four Indians. Dolop Singh. Jagat Singh, Mullah Singh, and Basanti Singh. According to the collective testimony of a group of "loyal" Indians, present at a meeting at the Sikh temple at 1866 Second Avenue West on December 27, 1913, Mr. H. Rahim, a prominent activist who had been subject to a number of unsuccessful deportation efforts, requested that someone "present in the audience . . . fix the three or four traitorous Hindus who are in league with the immigration authorities of this Province." Bela Singh later complained that at "pretty near every meeting in the temple . . . everybody lectured against me . . . and against Mr. Hopkinson and Mr. Reid. . . ." According to Bela, the priest Bhag Singh said: "Don't blame anything to the white people until you finish the Hindus who are doing service to the immigration authorities. Better tell them to cut away from the authorities, if they want money, we can pay them money; if they don't stop, then fix them some other way."

As the feud heated, Bela Singh and his cronies were ostracized, assaulted, and hounded inside and outside the temple and courts. A regular temple attendant before Bhagwan Singh's deportation, Bela stayed away from the meetings because "everybody against me." He quarreled with a man named Chewa and received a broken finger. At Victoria's harbor, he traded blows with a mob of assailants. Mr. Agaze Singh, a friend of the priest Bhag Singh, received a two-month prison sentence for assaulting Bela. According to a signed statement by "loyal" Indians, Mr. Chajoo Ram, a Pender Alley storekeeper whose window was broken on New Year's Eve, laid information against Bela's friend Baboo who "did not break the window. . . ." "I know the man who did break the window," the loyalists quoted Chajoo, "but I only laid this information against Baboo Singh to help our countrymen because he is opposed to our interests and because he is helping the immigration authorities against our interests. . . . I will keep after him and I will get him eventually. . . . I do not care what I do." In the winter and spring months of 1914, the court rolls filled with perjury and assault cases between Singh and Singh. In one case, the temple president, Mr. Bhag Singh, muttered "full Sikh Granth prayers in court and sprinkled holy water from India's River Ganges" for the entertainment of the judge. before testifying in his own defense on a charge of perjury. "During the swearing of the witnesses," Mr. I. M. Muthana, a local historian, noted. "some swore in one way and some in other ways and thus the men seemed to have not been following any order or discipline among themselves."

In the midst of these queer swearings and odd appearances, there drifted into Vancouver's harbor, on a cloudy May day in 1914, a creaky, rust-streaked ocean liner, bulging with eager Sikhs; a ship of destiny whose quest for a landing on the coast of white Canada lighted the fires of colonial resentment in India and converted a plethora of street and court fights among Vancouver's immigrant kin into a bloody vendetta. The voyage of the *Komagata Maru* was the brainchild of a Sikh patriot and businessman, Gurdit Singh, who dabbled in assorted businesses in India and the Malay states, before contemplating, in the Gurdwara of Hong Kong, the sad plight of Sikhs waiting in vain for transport to the New World. Moved by the orphaned state of his landless kin and attracted by the prospects of profit, Gurdit Singh collected passage fees from prospective passengers in Hong Kong, chartered a Glasgow-built vessel from a German agent employed by the owners of a Japanese firm. and picked up passengers and cargo along the way in Shanghai, Kobe. and Yokohama, before setting sail across the Pacific for the distant port of Vancouver.

Now Gurdit Singh was no mere adventurer. He had done some useful homework before chartering the vessel and had heard from a prominent firm of Hong Kong lawyers that there would be no problem in leaving the British colony with his human cargo, despite contrary indications and threats from the British authorities. Nor was he unaware of the *Panama Maru*'s recent successful run through Canada's immigration gauntlet, which, from the distant vantage of Hong Kong, seemed in a state of disarray. There was no reason, he surmised, why he should not attempt to emulate the *Panama Maru* and, in a bold act of patriotism and entrepreneurship, empty the Gurdwaras of Hong Kong and other port cities, as a prelude, perhaps, to ferrying, in a regular service, thousands more of the indigent Indians to the lush pastures and dusty sawmills of British Columbia. For Gurdit Singh, it was a special business venture fraught, it is true, with financial and political risk, but likely to yield a measure of patriotic satisfaction, if not financial profit.

103

Gurdit's vision, unfortunately, was not shared by the Canadian authorities, who, long before the *Komagata Maru*'s departure, were apprised of Gurdit's "seditious" intent and prepared to deal unflinchingly with the challenge posed by the ship's arrival. In their determination to bar entry and inflame opinion on ship, at home, and abroad, the authorities were well fortified. Following Chief Justice Hunter's *Panama Maru* decision, a trio of measures were passed — either unknown to Gurdit, or ignored in the hope or belief they could be bypassed — plugging loopholes in the law. The continuous-journey and $200-entry orders were reenacted to conform more closely with the Immigration Act, and a further order was passed that, in view of the "overcrowded conditions" of the labor market in British Columbia, made it illegal for artisans or laborers, skilled or unskilled, "to land at any port of entry in that province." There was, in addition, Section 23 of the Immigration Act, which barred appeals to the courts arising from decisions taken by immigration officials. Behind these regulations, and the minions that applied them, rested a solid phalanx of opinion, from the Conservative prime minister of Canada, Robert Borden, who closely monitored the entire affair, to the rowdies of Matt Sloper's Grandview Hotel bar, opposite the C.P.R. station, who were ready to take to the streets or wharves to halt the turbaned tide. Trade unions, church bodies, boards of trade, and politicians of all stripes and from every level of government joined in unison to oppose the "raghead invasion"; a chorus whipped into frenzy by the west-coast press, which ran inflammatory reports and editorials long before the arrival of the *Komagata Maru*, warning of the troubles ahead. "To admit Orientals in large numbers would mean in the end the extinction of the white peoples," Premier Sir Richard McBride said, echoing the views of his constituents, "and we have always in mind the necessity of keeping this a white man's country."[10]

It was really no contest, although the Indians on boat and shore fought the case valiantly. While the *Komagata Maru* and its human cargo remained anchored offshore for weeks, a lawyer was retained, Mr. J. Edward Bird, who maneuvered feverishly in an effort to replicate the success of the *Panama Maru*. Petitions were sent off to the king and the duke of Connaught; to the Indian viceroy, Lord Hardinge; and to Indian leaders in India and England. Food and supplies for the starving

---

10. Quoted in the *Times* (London), May 23, 1914. There were, to be sure, minor currents of opinion favorable to the "Hindus." These included some Quakers, a few Socialists, and gentlemen such as Mr. Wallace Wright who wrote in the June 17, 1914, edition of the *Vancouver News Advertiser*, "the Dominion has admitted and is admitting many most undesirable Europeans, Galicians, Armenians, Dukhobors, etc., yet we are keeping out men of tried loyalty who have fought for our empire in many climes and arduous campaigns."

passengers on the marooned ship were purchased and delivered at intervals, on approved launches. In a series of meetings, a "shore committee" was formed to collect monies, provision the passengers, and conduct the legal battle. The ship's charter was eventually assigned to two activists, Balwant Singh and Hussein Rahim, who, with their colleagues, paid off the monies demanded by the pressing agent of the chartering firm out of $22,000 that had been pledged at support meetings."[11] As tension heightened in the later stages of the ship's siege, three activists, Bhag Singh, Balwant Singh, and Mewa Singh, visited Abbotsford, crossed over the American border at Sumas, Washington, and purchased a supply of weapons and ammunition, which they hoped to smuggle aboard ship. On his return, Mewa was arrested at the Sumas crossing; dispossessed of three bags of cartridges and a pair of guns, which he had concealed in his left armpit and in a sling alongside his leg; and eventually sentenced to sixty days or a fifty-dollar fine, on a reduced charge of carrying a concealed weapon.[12] The stocky mill-worker, who had immigrated to British Columbia in 1906 from the village of Lopoke in Amritsar and who worked at Fraser Mills, later insisted that Hopkinson and Reid pressed him, with promises of immunity or reduced charges, to implicate Bhag and Balwant Singh, "in order to disclose a whole plot in which these Hindus are concerned."

It mattered little. No "Hindu conspiracy" trial was needed to inflame opinion solidly opposed to the landing of the *Komagata Maru*'s suffocating cargo. While Messrs. W. B. A. Ritchie and Robie L. Reid, lawyers for the Immigration Department and the federal minister of justice, maneuvered in the court, Malcolm Reid and Hopkinson took charge of affairs outside. Following passage through the First Narrows on May 27, the ship was ordered to weigh anchor several hundred yards off shore, where it remained for two months. The *Komagata Maru* was effectively quarantined and surrounded by patrolling launches from the Harbour Patrol and Immigration Department, night and day during its entire stay. Although 22 of the 376 passengers were admitted after proving they had been domiciled, the remainder were prevented from coming ashore, pending the outcome of the court battle. For the rest, Messrs. Reid and Hopkinson scoured the waters aboard the immigration launch, the *Winamac;* chaired and translated at numerous meetings of the board of inquiry, which dragged its feet and reserved decisions in

---

11. Since the ship was not allowed to dock, Gurdit Singh could not unload a shipment of coal whose delivery and sale would have yielded some of the cash necessary to cover charter fees.

12. His fine and legal fees were paid by the Sikh Temple Committee. A smuggling charge that could have earned him ten years was not proceeded with, on the intervention of Hopkinson.

S.S. Komagata Maru *in Vancouver Harbour, July 21, 1914. Provincial Archives of British Columbia*

numerous cases; closely consulted with legal advisors; reported regularly to their superiors; negotiated with Gurdit Singh and his colleagues through a tortuous process of boarding patrol launches; and maintained a useful espionage system on and off the ship, through men like Dr. Raghunath Singh, a surgeon recruited by Gurdit Singh in Hong Hong.

The momentous decision of the British Columbia Court of Appeal came on July 6, almost six weeks after the *Komagata Maru's* arrival in Vancouver. In the case of *Munshi Singh*, the learned judges refused a writ of habeas corpus, confirmed the validity of the orders-in-council on which the Immigration Department based its board of inquiry, and held that the controversial Section 23 of the Immigration Act was within the power of the government of Canada to enact. White Canada's firm stand and the dedication of her immigration minions had been rewarded. But Messrs. Reid and Hopkinson were not yet done. Although defeated in the courts, the *Komagata Maru* passengers refused to sail unless ample provisions for the return voyage were supplied by the Canadian government, and the shore committee compensated for their substantial outlays. For thirteen more days, Reid and Hopkinson patrolled the waters in their launch; cajoled and negotiated with Gurdit Singh; spied on the doings of the shore committee and ship's passengers; and threatened police and military action, following seizure of control of the ship from the Japanese captain, T. Yamamoto, who subsequently applied for police assistance. At 1:15 A.M., Sunday, July 19, a combined force of about one hundred and sixty police and special immigration officers, backed up by the militia on shore, invaded the *Komagata Maru* in the launch, the *Sea Lion*, whose deck, unfortunately, stood fifteen feet below that of the outlaw Japanese vessel. Jeering at their invaders from above, the aroused passengers rained a shower of rock, coal, bricks, scrap iron, and garbage on the men below, causing several serious injuries and a hurried retreat to shore. But the invaders — about a hundred strong — returned two days later on the *Rainbow*, a 300-foot, 3,600-ton cruiser purchased several years before from the Royal Navy, which had been recommissioned at Esquimalt and, in 1914, constituted an entire half of Canada's naval fleet. Equipped with two six-inch and six four-inch guns and a collection of fire hoses, and manned by a crew sent all the way from Halifax, the *Rainbow* sailed out alongside the *Komagata Maru*, in full view of an admiring audience of white citizens on shore, who crowded the dock, roofs, and windows of adjoining buildings and waterfront bars to guzzle beer and share a common joy in the final countdown.[13] A contingent of land forces stood ready as a backup on shore, including men from the Irish Fusilliers, the 72nd Highlanders, and the 6th D.C.O.R.

No shore aid was needed. The agreement of the Honourable Martin Burrell — the federal minister of agriculture, who had been sent out to negotiate on behalf of the federal government — to launch an inquiry by an impartial commission into the shore committee's claims and to give sympathetic consideration to those who deserved "generous treatment," was enough, finally, to induce Gurdit Singh and his followers to relent. At dawn on July 23, a full two months after her arrival, the *Komagata Maru* fired her boilers, lifted anchor, and painfully lumbered westward out of Burrard Inlet, towards distant Asian ports where, unfortunately, further tribulations awaited her in succeeding months.

Considering the length of her stay and the heat of the emotions generated, the *Komagata Maru*'s Canadian visit had been a remarkably bloodless affair; a tribute, no doubt, to the restraint of the passengers and their leader and to the prudence of shore officials like Hopkinson, who remained "cool, calm and collected," a *Province* reporter concluded, "in many situations which may have developed into tragedy." Succeeding

---

13. According to Rear Admiral Hose, at least one of the *Komagata Maru* passengers had a sense of humor; an old white-bearded fellow who stood on the bridge as the *Rainbow* approached and executed a perfect semaphore signal that read, "Our only ammunition is coal."

events, however, proved considerably bloodier, in India as well as British Columbia. Treated as a pariah in Canadian waters, the *Komagata Maru* was shunned at Hong Kong, Kobe, Yokohama, and Singapore, where British officials, embroiled in a world war and nervous about the possibly unsettling effects of the ship's arrival on the local Sikh soldiery, blocked the landing of her notorious cargo.

It was not until September 29, that the *Komagata Maru* finally berthed in India, at Budge Budge Harbour, at the mouth of the Hooghly River near Calcutta, where Gurdit Singh and his men were met by a contingent of police, acting on the authority of the Ingress Ordinance of 1914, which restricted the freedom of movement of anyone entering India after September 5, 1914. When ordered by the police to board a train for the Punjab, the men refused and, carrying a Sikh flag and copy of the Holy Granth at the head of their procession, began marching for Hooghly. The police intercepted them and began firing. In the ensuing battle, nineteen of the passengers died, and twenty-five were wounded. Three police and two spectators died as well.[14]

In Vancouver, meanwhile, past feuds among the local Indians, exacerbated by the *Komagata Maru*'s galling stay, erupted into a bloody vendetta. The settling of accounts began with Mr. Harnam Singh, a friend and collaborator of Bela Singh, who had given evidence favorable to Bela during one of the many court cases against him. Harnam disappeared from his home in mid-August. When his body was discovered several weeks later on the Kitsilano Indian Reserve, with his jugular severed, it was rumored that he had committed suicide, though why he would bother binding his legs in his turban before doing so remained a mystery of Himalayan proportions.

Arjan Singh's demise, on September 5, was equally suspicious. An associate of Bela's, Arjan was found dead on the floor of a Sikh rooming house with a bullet wound in his neck. The police subsequently found a revolver and box of cartridges belonging to the dead man hidden in a garbage can in a corner of the yard behind the house. There were friends, or enemies, of Arjan present when he died, but they could not agree on causes and events. While it was established that Ram Singh, a member of an opposite faction, had fired the bullet, it was not certain that he had done so intentionally. The jury at a subsequent trial concluded that it had been accidental and that Ram had merely been trying to show Arjan how the gun worked, when it went off.

---

14. Gurdit Singh escaped. It took the authorities weeks to round up the bulk of the passengers, two hundred of whom were shipped to the Punjab and interned under the authority of the Ingress Ordinance. Fired by the prospect of revolution at home, boatloads of Ghadarites returned to India, including a thousand from North America, and spread the mutiny message among the Sikh soldiery and in towns and villages in the Punjab and beyond.

All of this was not taken lightly by Bela, who decided to take his private war with the radicals to the very foot of the altar of the Kitsilano Gurdwara. Following the cremation and burial of Arjan Singh, Bela ended his long absence from the Gurdwara by attending obsequial services for the dead man. He entered the temple on Second Avenue West, at around 7 P.M., removed his shoes, contributed to the offertory, and knelt behind the temple president and priest, Bhagwan Singh. It was in the midst of prayer, following the singing of the hymn, that matters got out of hand. Again, there were different stories among those present — around thirty or forty in number — as to what happened. Bela and his friends insisted that he was taunted as an "immigrant dog" and threatened by Bhagwan Singh, wielding the sacred sword, and by Buttan Singh, with a pistol. Bela's enemies denied any provocation. Bela, in any event, decided to let fly, seized a pair of pistols from under his coat, and fired two quick shots, then a fusillade, killing Bhagwan Singh and Buttan Singh and injuring several others. More casualties resulted from a stampede out of the back door when several frantic congregants crashed over the porch railing and fell sixteen feet to the ground. When the police arrived, they found trails of blood leading in every direction outside and a contingent of survivors at the door of the Gurdwara ready to bar their entry pending removal of their shoes, as an act of respect for the sanctity of the holy edifice. "Inspector Scott, however, thought that the temple had already been desecrated by the blood spilled on the costly rugs and spattered over the altar," the *Sun* sourly noted. "He did not wait for the ceremony."

Following his mad reckoning, Bela Singh made no attempt to flee or hide his deed and calmly surrendered to the police at the Kitsilano station. When probed about the causes of his outburst by a Constable Lemon, who later gave evidence at a preliminary hearing, Bela merely replied: "I shoot. Inspectors Reid and Hopkinson, they know."

Unfortunately, neither the learned counsel for the prosecution or for the defense had a chance to examine Mr. Hopkinson about Bela's intentions. While relaxing, hands in trouser pockets, against the wall of the corridor outside the witness room on the second floor of Vancouver's main courthouse, on Tuesday morning, October 21, Hopkinson was approached by a stocky, fleshy Sikh in a dark suit, a friend and political associate of the dead priest, Bhagwan Singh. Without uttering a word, Mewa Singh, the radical arrested on a gun-smuggling charge during the *Komagata Maru*'s stay, drew a pair of guns from under his coat and, before an astonished audience of his Indian peers and several witnesses waiting, like Mr. Hopkinson, to testify, began firing into Mr. Hopkinson's chest, a few inches away. Hopkinson fell to his knees after the first shot, rose momentarily and grappled with his assailant, then succumbed

109

after three more shots and a clubbing on the head with a revolver butt. He collapsed and fell over on his back, with his body in the corridor and his head protruding into the witness room. When a pair of detectives and the court janitor arrived at the scene, they found several frightened Indians running for the exit and Mewa Singh still standing over his groaning victim, who died within half an hour. Mewa was quickly disarmed by janitor James McCann, who had been busy raising the flag outside for Trafalgar Day when the shots came. "I shoot. I don't care" was all Mewa Singh volunteered before removal to the central police station.

The citizens of Vancouver did care and accorded the late W. C. Hopkinson, a loyal servant of British India and white Canada, a martyr's burial. While the body lay in state in the decorated marble corridor of the Cordova Street police station, several thousand Vancouverites gathered outside to show their respect for the deceased and sympathy for his widow and children. After the presiding minister recited prayers, read from the scriptures, and spoke "briefly and appropriately of the life and example of the man who had died while doing his duty," the First Presbyterian Church choir rendered "Nearer My God To Thee" and "Abide With Me" in concert with the crowd outside, whose chorus could be heard several blocks away. The procession through the city's core to Mountainview Cemetery included a corps of mounted police, a 6th Regiment band and "C" Company to which the deceased belonged, 130 policemen, 100 firemen, several hundred members of the Orange Lodge, as well as officials from the Canadian and American immigration services, the C.P.R. police, the post office, and the customs service. A Mr. A. D. Kean, known as the "Cowboy Photographer of B.C.," took films of the funeral, which were subsequently shown at a local theater and offered for sale to the Immigration Department for twenty dollars. "I am sure the revolutionary party would purchase the film," Mr. R. J. Reid wrote to W. W. Cory, deputy minister of the interior, "if they knew it was for sale." While Mr. Cory spurned the film offer, he did agree to cover the full cost of the elaborate funeral with departmental funds.

In W. C. Hopkinson, British Columbia's white community had won a martyr; the Sikhs gained theirs in the person of Mewa Singh. Mewa's trial, held a few days after Hopkinson's burial, in a courtroom within feet of the place of the murder, was brief, without frills. It lasted an hour and forty-five minutes, some sort of record in recent British Columbia legal history for a murder trial. The jury deliberated a mere five minutes. At Mewa's insistence, the defense presented no witnesses and waived cross-examination of the few presented by the Crown. In the witness box, Mewa confessed, even proclaimed his guilt, as he did at the trial's commencement. But he insisted that his counsel, a Mr. E. M. Woods,

Mewa Singh.

read a prepared statement in which he deplored the desecration of his temple and the sufferings inflicted on his people by men like Hopkinson, Bela Singh, and Malcolm Reid. Mewa insisted that Hopkinson and his colleagues had harrassed and pressured him to testify against his colleagues throughout the *Komagata Maru*'s stay. As a God-fearing man, who prayed every morning for an hour and for a further half hour at night, he "shot Mr. Hopkinson out of honour and principle to my fellow man and my religion . . . it is better for a Sikh to die than to bring such disgrace and ill-treatment in the temple." Following this statement, Mewa requested that the orphaned daughters of Bhagwan Singh be brought into the court to hear what he had to say. When the children could not be located, he startled the court spectators, only four of whom were Sikhs, all carefully frisked before entry, by breaking into a religious chant. "He wishes you to know," a court interpreter announced following the chant's conclusion, "that the words he has sung are from the Sikh scriptures and say that it is the duty of a good man to give his life for a good cause and that the condition of the Hindus in Vancouver is as bad as when the Mohammedans ruled India."

Mewa's outburst had little impact on the jurors, who took only minutes to arrive at a guilty verdict and recommend that "both Dominion and Provincial authorities formulate some plan for the better protection of those brave officers whose duty calls upon them to risk their persons in defence of law and order. We specially recommend special attention be paid to watching 'Hindus' and other foreigners. . . . " When Mewa asked Mr. Justice Morrison for mercy, since he had killed "in a good cause," the judge replied, "it is beyond my power to do anything save pronounce the sentence the law attaches to crimes of this description." The hanging was set for January 11, 1915, in the provincial jail at New Westminster where, in the early dawn hours of that fateful day, the priest Balwan Singh entered Mewa's cell and joined him in a final chant. "In performing the duty of a true Sikh and remembering the name of God," Mewa announced in his scaffold speech: "[I] proceed towards the scaffold with the same amount of pleasure as a hungry babe does towards its mother. I shall gladly have the rope put around my neck thinking it to be a rosary of God's name. I am quite sure that God will take me into his blissful arms as I have not done this deed for my personal interests but to the benefit of my people and the Canadian government."

Over three hundred and fifty Indians in procession, marching five abreast, accompanied Mewa's body the four miles to Fraser Mills, where it was burnt on a pyre according to Sikh rites. Soon afterwards, Mewa's portrait, his scaffold speech, and his final letters, adorned with glowing accounts of his martyrdom, began circulating in the Gurdwaras across

North America in publications like the *Khalsa Shamsher* of Stockton, California, which observed, in a commemorative issue, that the martyred Sikh had gained ten pounds during his imprisonment and interpreted this as proof of his courage, convictions, and indifference to worldly punishment. "The death which ordinary mortals dread," the *Shamsher* concluded, "is a source of pleasure to patriots, such men face the scaffold unflinchingly and without complaint or regret." Henceforth, the anniversary of Mewa Singh's execution was revered and celebrated throughout the Indian immigrant communities as Mewa Singh Martyr Day.[15]

Bela Singh, understandably, did not share Mewa's martyrdom. Interrupted by Hopkinson's death and Mewa's trial, Bela's ordeal began in earnest in early November. Hopkinson's death, while doubtless mourned by Bela, added a new and favorable perspective to his case. Bela's lawyer, a Mr. E. J. McDougall, argued forcefully that his client had escaped his friend's fate only by killing in self-defense, after reasonably perceiving a present danger. While prosecution witnesses averred that Bela had not been threatened or provoked in any way before or after entering the temple, the defense countered with its own people, political friends of Bela, some in the employ of the Immigration Department, who supported Bela's claim that he had been harrassed and threatened for months preceding the September fifth Gurdwara meeting, as well as during the service itself. In his own defense, Bela read from the *Ghadar* to prove the seditious and murderous intent of his enemies and insisted that he had been assaulted and threatened numerous times before, during, and after the *Komagata Maru* affair as well as during the evening of his outburst, when Bhag Singh and his colleagues arranged to have the back door of the temple locked, as a prelude to killing him.

Bela's plea was forceful enough to result in a hung jury. At a retrial, however, the jurors took their cue from Mr. Justice Morrison, whose charge left little doubt about his own feelings. "The prisoner should hardly be tested by our standards," His Lordship stated, "and in view of the fact that they were Hindus and all by themselves in a strange country and ridden by hopeless feuds. The prisoner was one of the men who stood for law and order, while the opposite side was preaching sedition and importing seditious literature and trying to undermine British rule within the Empire. It is a wonder to me that the authorities are allowing it. The prisoner and his side are trying to stop it, but some have been killed and threats were made to kill the prisoner. They threatened and

---

15. The British authorities were understandably upset at Mewa's instant martyrdom and the attendant publicity and regretted the "supineness of the authorities of California in allowing the executed murderer of a Canadian official to be introduced to the public as a martyr."

killed Inspector Hopkinson, and if they could shoot him right in the corridors of the court house, how much easier must they have thought it to kill the prisoner when in the Temple." The acquittal was assured and was welcomed by Mr. Justice Morrison, who, after ordering the prisoner released, urged him "to try to forget such things and after it is over, do not endeavour to get even. . . . I trust that you will continue as heretofore and assist in preserving peace and order and suppressing those who conspire against them."

Bela, it seems, took the acquittal, and Judge Morrison's exhortation, as a vindication of his old ways and, after celebrating with friends, resumed where he had left off. While, in the distant Punjab, the Ghadarites and their radical allies looted moneylender's shops, murdered informers, derailed trains, raided military outposts, and plotted an army mutiny, their Vancouver kin played out the final act of their own ugly feuds.[16] When Jagat Singh, new to the game of shoving and fighting, was placed on trial in March for shooting Rattan Singh, an ally of Bela's, he informed the court that it was Bela who had supplied the gun and ammunition and who had offered a bribe in order to get a pair of old enemies out of the way — a charge denied by Bela. Jagat, in any event, either changed his heart or his aim, or was confused by the effect of liquor, which figured during the trial. He was sentenced to four years, and had barely begun his term when a load of dynamite set under the verandah of a home on Second Avenue West, owned by a Mutab Singh, a friend of Bela's, exploded, tore out the whole front porch and the corner of the house, and showered the entire block with debris, killing the owner and severely injuring two of his colleagues. The culprits were never found. Several days later, Bela returned to direct action and, with a pair of cronies, pummelled one Lachman Singh into senselessness. Bela's creditability finally ran out and the judge who heard the case in June, 1915, sentenced him and his colleague, Bhagat Singh, to a year's imprisonment.[17] Two others involved in the fracas, Sewa Singh and Naina Singh, were given six months each.

With Bela in prison, where he was "considerately treated as he had

---

16. Of 291 tried in the Lahore conspiracy and the supplementary trials that followed the failure of the coup in August, 1915, 42 were sentenced to death and hanged, 114 transported for life, and 93 imprisoned. Among those hanged was Balwant Singh, the Vancouver priest who had returned to India with other North American Ghadarites to spread the mutiny message.

17. The presiding judge likely supported the view of Mr. H.M. Clogstoun who investigated the claims of the Shore Committee following the *Komagata Maru* affair. "From what I have seen," Clogstoun wrote, "there is morally no difference between some of the so-called 'loyal' men . . . who discredit the department employing them by using their connections to terrorize their fellow Indians for their own ends, and the disloyal or openly seditious persons who exploit their fellows. . . ."

been helpful with the loyal elements," the feuding died except for a brief lapse in Abbotsford where in October, 1915, a Mit Singh Pandori was fired on by a Partab Singh, a friend of Bela's. Partab missed and, in turn, was pummelled so mercilessly by Mit's friends that he was hospitalized and nearly died. After his own release, Bela quietly returned to India with the blessing of the Immigration Department and dropped from Vancouver's court rolls and public gaze for nearly two decades.[18] In May, 1934, however, a report appeared on the wires about a gruesome murder outside the village of Jaina in the Punjab, where a local resident, formerly "considered to be the handsomest Sikh in British Columbia," had his arms, legs, and head hacked off by an unknown assailant. Bela Singh, at last, had earned his due and been dispatched by agents of the Babbar Akali, a terrorist outgrowth of the *Ghadar*, to a realm that to this day knows no passports or quotas.

---

18. The Hindu vendetta drama in the late war years shifted from British Columbia to San Francisco. There, during the "German-Hindu" conspiracy trials, which began in November, 1917, Ram Chandra, a radical editor, was shot dead at the foot of the witness stand by Ram Singh, formerly of British Columbia. Ram Singh, in turn, was killed by a United States marshall. In all, twenty-nine persons were found guilty, including Taraknath Das and Bhagwan Singh, who were sentenced to twenty-two and eighteen months respectively on McNeil's Island.

5
THE ARCTIC CIRCLE WAR

To Constable Alfred W. "Buns" King of the Royal Canadian Mounted Police, it was purely a routine matter, without the slightest prospect of epic. He was standing there, at the door of a small cabin, near the mouth of the Rat River, in the blowing snows of Canada's western Arctic, to investigate complaints by several Loucheux Indians that their trap lines had been interfered with by a surly Scandinavian who later came to be known as Albert Johnson.

The cabin, Constable King observed, was a small, solid structure, about eight feet by ten, with walls built of foot-wide logs. The roof was packed with a thick layer of sod and frozen snow, and the doorway stood about four feet high. At intervals along the walls and close to the base, which was reinforced to a height of three feet by a second layer of logs, were a series of loopholes wide enough to admit the muzzle of a rifle. The cellophane window in front was covered over by a piece of cloth, which prevented King from peeking inside and observing the occupant whose queer reticence kept the constable standing for an hour in the forty-degree-below-zero cold.

Constable King had been warned about the hermetic antipathies of Albert Johnson, who had first appeared, in July 1931, outside Fort McPherson — a small trading fort operated by Northern Traders Limited consisting of 250 souls, several whitewashed shacks, and a batch of Indians — on a raft, floating down the Peel River. Slightly stooped, of moderate height, with sandy hair, blue eyes, a snub nose, and Swedish accent, Johnson arrived in town with only a few possessions: a rifle, a mosquito net, and a small pack. But he owned a wad of bills and spent freely at W. W. Douglas's Northern Traders Limited trading post, where he loaded up with supplies, including a single barrel shotgun and shells, and evaded the questions of curious local residents who, observing a stranger in town, were keen to know his particulars. When Constable Edgar (Spike) Millen of the Arctic Red River detachment of the

R.C.M.P. arrived at the fort, questioned Johnson about his intentions, and offered to sell him a trapping licence, he also met with a surly silence. Johnson, it seemed, was not interested in socializing and soon drifted away, in a canoe purchased from a local Indian, towards the Rat River. Here, on a promontory at a sharp bend near the river's mouth, not far from a spot known as Destruction City, where a party of overlanders had lost their loot and equipment to the rapids in 1898, Johnson constructed his lonesome fortress, bounded on three sides by the raging river. From this base, he waged his silent war on the local Indians.

Johnson was home on that frigid day, December 28, 1931, when Constable King arrived. "I spent nearly an hour at the cabin," King complained, "knocking on the door and calling to Johnson and informed him who I was and that I wished to speak to him, but he refused to open the door or answer." In a subsequent report King wrote, "I saw him peeping at me through the small window near the door, which he immediately covered when he saw me looking at him." King's requests to enter and speak with the occupant met with a silence so strange that he withdrew in frustration and drove his dog team eighty miles down the Husky River to Aklavik, a town of 230 Indians, Eskimos, and whites, which served as the sub-district headqarters of the R.C.M.P.

When King informed Commanding Officer A. N. Eames of his misadventure, the inspector sensed trouble and provided King with a search warrant, a set of dogs, a toboggan, guns, ammunition, and several aides, including a pair of Indian special constables and Constable R. G. McDowell. The officers returned to the field immediately, and after a day of marching in sub-zero weather, they arrived back at Johnson's cabin, which, King noted on approach, was still occupied.

King again parked at the door, importuned with Johnson, reminded him of the warrant, warned of the consequences of further resistance. When King seized an ax to knock the door down, Johnson finally replied — with a rifle shot through the door that hit the constable in the chest. While King lay bleeding in the snow, Officer McDowell, under the cover of a nearby thicket of willows, seized a rifle from the sled and opened fire on the cabin. King managed to crawl away to the safety of the river bank and was helped by McDowell onto the toboggan, which carried him during a twenty-hour run through howling blizzards back to Aklavik and the tender care of the acting assistant surgeon at the Anglican mission hospital. King survived the ordeal and was released to resume his duties several weeks later.

McDowell's return run with the wounded cargo, advertised by the *Edmonton Bulletin* as "another epic of the famous force," inspired Inspector Eames to muster and outfit a full expedition to bring the demented hermit to justice. The constable collected Eskimo auxiliaries, Indian dog drivers, several Scandinavian trappers, and a collection of forty-two dogs divided into six teams. Toboggans were loaded with food, ammunition, and a cache of dynamite, together with caps and fuses. Near the mouth of the Rat, the expedition was joined by Constable Edgar Millen who had picked up a radio message broadcast by UZK Aklavik, "Voice of the Northern Lights," an amateur station run by army signalers.

Unfortunately, Inspector Eames's Rat River expedition proved less efficient than McDowell's return run. Trapper Charlie Rat, who had enlisted as a guide following New Year's celebrations at Fort McPherson, took the men on an exotic circular route, causing them to confound their directions, circle aimlessly, and lose a precious two days. Oddly enough, when the Mounties did finally arrive at Johnson's abode, ten days after leaving Aklavik, they found him at home, clattering his dishes, and tending to domestic chores. The posse approached stealthily. After tying the dogs to the trees along the riverbed, they crawled up to the cabin and surrounded it on three sides. The inspector called to Johnson, told him that he was surrounded, and assured him that King had not died. Johnson, as ever, remained silent. Anticipating a lengthy siege and troubled by a food supply that had dwindled to two day's rations, Inspector Eames ordered his troops into action. Several police and trappers rushed the door but were driven off by gunfire through the cabin's loopholes. When two of the attacking party began bashing in the door with their rifle butts, Johnson, positioned in a dugout trench with a gun in each hand, let loose with a renewed spurt of fire.

Inspector Eames knew this would be no easy job. A camp was struck on the riverbed nearby and fires lit. While the dynamite thawed out, the officers approached Johnson again, pleaded with him, circled, and traded fire. At nine o'clock in the evening, several sticks of explosive were hurled against the cabin, where they went off without effect. A lob onto the roof succeeded in blowing a small hole in the cabin's ceiling. By midnight, the men were irritable, freezing, hungry, and suffering from a lack of sleep due to the howling of the restive dogs. At 3 A.M., Inspector Eames launched a final desperate attack. Four pounds of dynamite were thrown at the door, blowing it open. Inspector Eames and trapper Carl Gardlund then charged for the entrance door, armed with guns and a flashlight, which Johnson, prone in a pit, shot from Gardlund's hand.

The officers retreated and, after an hour's nap, set out with their entire party for Aklavik, where they announced the failure of their second expedition. But Inspector Eames was not to be deterred. He immediately dispatched an advance party, consisting of Constable Millen and trapper Gardlund, to a location two miles from Johnson's cabin, charged with observing and reporting Johnson's activities. Meanwhile, the constable set to work organizing a bigger and better attack force. Ammunition and food were collected; bombs fashioned from dynamite, beer bottles, and cylinders of dismantled engines; and a two-way wireless radio readied for transport on a toboggan. On January 16, a motley force of constables, Indians, and trappers — including the Royal Canadian Signal Corps wireless operator R. F. Riddel — left with the usual contingent of dogs for the mouth of the Rat River.

When Eames's party arrived the next day, they were greeted by an Indian who relayed a message from the advance patrol that Albert Johnson had finally fled from his cabin. Augmented by an auxiliary force of eleven Indians, Eames's force continued downstream where they surveyed the area of the deserted cabin, then joined up with the advance patrol and pitched camp along the river nine miles above the cabin. During the next few days, the search party scoured the entire Rat canyon for twenty miles, visited several deserted cabins, and explored the vicinity of Johnson's trap lines.

Johnson was not far away, but the invading army, braving fierce storms and plummeting temperatures, could not get near him. Traveling by foot, alone, without the aid or sympathy of local trappers and Indians. Johnson stuck to the hard-packed snow of high ridges or to frozen riverbeds swept free of snow by raging winds. Equipped with snowshoes and feeding off several caches he had laid away for the winter, as well as on the occasional snared squirrel or rabbit, he carried his world on his back and succeeded in confounding his pursuers who, after three days of wandering along riverbeds polished by wind-driven snow and resembling great sheets of plate glass, packed it in. After comtemplating his meager supplies, Inspector Eames dismissed the Indian auxiliaries and, concluding that the remaining force was still too large to sustain, led a party of weary men back to distant Aklavik. Constables E. Millen, Noel Verville, Carl Gardlund, and Q.M. Sergeant Riddell remained in the field, with the radio and enough supplies for nine days.

While Inspector Eames mustered a new contingent in Aklavik, and the radio waves throughout the frozen north beamed the news of the determined flight of the Mad Trapper. Constable Millen's party doggedly pursued Johnson's faint and intermittent trail. They discovered several of his old camps, stumbled on caches, and picked up a few clues from local Indians, one of whom reported having heard the sound of a gunshot near the Bear River, on January 28. The party went to investigate and, after a day of roaming around the confluence of the Rat and Barrier rivers, suddenly came upon a camp set behind a barricade of trees alongside a creek bed.

The search party split. While Officers Gardlund and Riddell located themselves on the bank opposite the camp. Constables Millen and Verville descended along the hill into the creek and approached the camp of Albert Johnson who, between coughs audible to the officers along the bank, snapped off a quick shot that barely missed Millen. The officers replied with a fusillade in the direction of the improvised fortress, built of spruce logs crisscrossed over one another and packed with snow. When no return fire came during the next few hours, Constable Millen and Sergeant Riddell, sensing that their man had been hurt or killed in the earlier exchange, forced the issue and advanced slowly towards the barricade. They were no more than twenty feet away when Johnson fired and missed. Millen shot back and was struck in the chest by a bullet. Under the protective fire of Verville, Sergeant Riddell crawled out to rescue Millen and managed to drag his motionless body up the steep bank into the clump of spruce trees. Constable Millen, it was discovered, was dead.

It was not long before the news of the Mountie killing, and Johnson's mad-dog stand, reached Aklavik where Inspector Eames ordered a full mobilization in preparation for a renewed assault. The *Edmonton Bulletin*'s Arctic war correspondent reported that a trapper army was contemplated, to be mobilized by radio through appeals to the myriad isolated cabins dotting the Mackenzie District of the Northwest Territories and the neighboring Yukon. The Royal Canadian Signal Corps telegraph station broadcast the news to Edmonton, where Superintendent A. E. Acland, commanding the Sixth Division of the R.C.M.P. force, concluded that new equipment, reinforcements, and tactics were necessary. Acland contacted Major General J. H. MacBrien, commissioner of the Royal Canadian Mounted Police in Ottawa who, after meeting with the federal justice minister, the Honourable Hugh Guthrie, agreed to lend air power to the forces at the front. Several days later, a Bellanca single-prop airplane, leased from Western Canada Airways, with room for five people and piloted by C. H. (Punch) Dickens, flew out of Edmonton 200 miles to Fort McMurray, carrying a supply of munitions, tear gas, and several police officers. At Fort McMurray the plane was met by a Fokker, flown by one of the aces of Canada's military and civic aviation, Captain Wilfred Reid (Wop) May, a combatant of Baron von Richthofen over the Amiens front in France in 1918 and recipient of the Distinguished Flying Cross and assorted war service medals. In his post-war years, May served as a pioneer bush pilot specializing in mail runs, mercy missions, and commercial flights from northern Alberta to the sub-Arctic regions of the Mackenzie delta.

When it was heard that Wop May had joined the fray, there was rejoicing in the Arctic and elation in the editorial offices of the *Edmonton Free Press*, where the idea of dropping bombs on the crazed hermit's

Wop May. R.C.M.P. Archives

makeshift barricade was heatedly debated, then rejected, after consideration. "Technical difficulties will prevent bombs being used from a modern commercial cabin plane," a reporter volunteered, "unless a hole is sawn in the floor. The single side door needs two men to open it against the force of the propeller slip-stream, and there will hardly be room for another man to do any calculating and then hurl a bomb between the two crouching at the door."

Wop May, it appeared, came to the same general conclusion and refused to do any bombing lest the tail of the Fokker be blown off. His arrival at Aklavik, following brief stopovers in Fort Simpson and Fort Norman, introduced a new and critical factor into the Arctic Circle war. Hitherto hampered by supply and transport problems and forced to rely on the uncertain shuttle service of exhausted dog teams, the Aklavik command now enjoyed a perfect aide and substitute — a cargo plane equipped to land on frozen ground and ice and piloted by an experienced northern pilot. May, as well, could perform reconnaissance functions and spy from his airborne vantage — weather conditions permitting — the

121

trail and movements of the snowshoed desperado. And he could ferry personnel from the front to headquarters and back, or transport casualties to the hospital. Among Wop May's first jobs after arriving in Aklavik was to fly out to the place of Constable Millen's death and return with the body to headquarters, a somber mission reported in full chromatic detail on the front page of the *Edmonton Bulletin* for February 10: "With its propeller chanting a funeral dirge as it swam out of the western haze, a blue and gold monoplane brought the body of a dead 'redcoat' back to the port from which he had mushed out two weeks ago to capture a red-handed outlaw."

The Fokker's arrival was a welcome accretion to the strength of the embattled forces of law and order. But the real war was fought below, if not in the trenches, then along snowdrifts, ice patches, frozen riverbeds, willow clumps, scrub spruce, and expanses of tundra, where Inspector Eames deployed a platoon of recruits in a final assault on the Mad Trapper. The problem, as Inspector Eames discovered on his return to the site of Johnson's Second Stand, was that the hermit would not sit still and disappeared from under the nose of his guards before the new expeditionary force arrived. "The whole of the day was spent in searching the ravine which is almost nine miles in length," one officer lamented. "We were now in the larger foothills, with numerous creeks in deep ravines and canyons, running from the watershed. Between the creeks were the frozen tundra, covered with snow made hard by the winds that seemed to blow without cessation, and always with a drift that obliterated snow-shoe tracks or footprints very quickly. Johnson's comparatively fresh tracks were found on February 6, 7 and 8 in three different creeks (four to six miles apart), showing that the fugitive had been crossing over the tundra from creek to creek, probably during the night, and always circling eight to ten miles back to his own track. A night patrol found his tracks, only a few hours old, on the Barrier River, but lost it again when it went up to the tundra."

The trapper was doubtless crazy — like an Arctic fox. "If he is demented," a weary Mounted Police officer commented, "we all ought to be." By mid-February, the war of endurance between the stooped hermit lugging a pack on his back and a platoon of parka-clad Mounties and their auxiliaries, upholding the finest tradition of the brave constabulary, had stretched into its sixth week and beyond the Great Divide. Following his Second Stand, Johnson, who could barely light a fire without being seen or shoot a caribou without being heard, undertook a trek which the local Indians thought impossible for a man traveling alone: he crossed, in the dead of winter, through the Richardson Mountains via McDougall Pass into the neighboring Yukon. Once there, he began trudging westward, towards Alaska, a mere 175 miles away.

But the trapper could not shake his pursuers who, strung out along the Barrier and Rat rivers, heard from an Indian courier that strange tracks had been sited near LaPierre House in the Yukon, a decrepit Hudson's Bay Company fort located along the old trail of '98, at the juncture of the Bell and Porcupine rivers. Augmented by Colonel S. W. May and several auxiliaries from the Old Crow Fort, who had picked up an appeal from the Dawson R.C.M.P. headquarters via the UZK station at Anchorage, Alaska, Inspector Eames deployed his forces across the border, where a base camp was set up at LaPierre House. Tired dog teams were dismissed and fresh ones put into service at LaPierre House. Indian recruits were replaced by new men, a replenishment that doubtless pleased the *Edmonton Bulletin*, still fighting the Arctic war from afar. "The noble red men with the posse," the *Bulletin* war correspondent commented, "have not qualified for any medals for distinguished conduct . . . they are right there when the cookhouse call is sounded, but missing when the guns begin to shoot. Loucheux Indians at LaPierre House [are] about the best Indians and trackers to be found on the continent. They are far superior to the nondescript types which hang around the lower MacKenzie."

Inspector Eames's new and old recruits, aided as ever by Wop May's reconnaissance and shuttle service — which trimmed the supply time from Rat River to Aklavik from twenty hours to one — concentrated their search southwest of LaPierre House, in the Porcupine District, along the Bell, Porcupine, and Eagle rivers. In choosing to cross the divide, the Mad Trapper had created some new problems for himself. There was little wind on the Yukon side, and the snowfall was heavier. His tracks were more visible to the search party and to Wop May, whose flight route was aided by markers dropped by the posse below. But Johnson trudged onward and resorted to old and new desperate ploys. When a caribou herd swept through the Eagle Basin, he removed his snowshoes, joined the migration and lost, during ten miles, his tracks among the thousand hooves. He stuck to ice and hard-snow patches, circling and backtracking endlessly, in order to place himself in a favorable position for observing or possibly ambushing his pursuers.

It was during one of these return trips along the bed of the Eagle River, that Albert Johnson noticed, to his consternation, the figure of a police officer, driving a team of dogs. The recognition, around the sharp bend in the river, at a distance of 250 yards, was mutual and the reaction instantaneous. Colonel E. F. Hersey, who drove the team at the head of the posse of eleven men and eight dog teams, was as surprised as Johnson by the meeting, since the tracks he was following seemed older than two days. But Officer Hersey did not bother pondering the matter. He shouted to his colleagues behind him, seized his gun from the toboggan, and began chasing Johnson, who ran for cover along the edge of the bank. Joined by Verville, Hersey ran to the center of the river bed, kneeled, and set himself for a shot. Too late. Johnson, without setting himself, fired on target and hit Hersey with a single bullet that exited through the officer's knee, elbow, and chest. While Verville tended to his wounded partner, the rest of the posse opened fire on their quarry, who turned and ran back along his own trail, in the center of the river. Stopping at intervals to fire at his pursuers, Johnson opened his lead to 500 yards, then fell to the ice, a bullet in his leg. Still he kept on fighting. As the posse closed on him, he burrowed into the snow, positioned his backpack to act as a shield, and fired a volley of shots. While May soared in his Fokker overhead, and peered down at the prone speck bedded in the snows of an Arctic creek, the men below poured a volley of fire into the tortured, squirming body of the outlaw. Johnson was in the midst of reloading his rifle when the fatal bullet struck. Taking no chances, the men waited a good while before edging up and claiming the hideous remains of that emaciated being, whose hatred and fear of capture, had known no bounds.

The quiet burial of Albert Johnson, following a brief inquest near Aklavik, attracted a few stragglers. But his desperate stand was never forgotten by the people of the north, or by the men of the Mounted Police, who had pursued him over the frozen tundra at the top of the

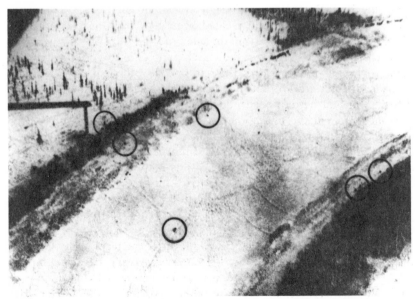

Aerial photograph of the shoot-out on the Eagle River. Johnson is in the middle of the river bed. R.C.M.P. Archives

world. "An unequal combat," the *Toronto Globe* editorialized, "a lone man fighting the forces of nature and the resources of a government . . . there could be but one ending to this tragic conflict, and it came suddenly and dramatically. . . . Silence again in the Arctic Circle. The law had been upheld. The Mounties had got their man."

But who had the Mounties killed? No two people agreed. The theories and letters poured in, for months and years: an outlaw known as the Blueberry Kid; a bush-crazed ex-Chicago gangster; a trapper called Arthur Nelson; a queer Canadian teamster; a farmhand from the

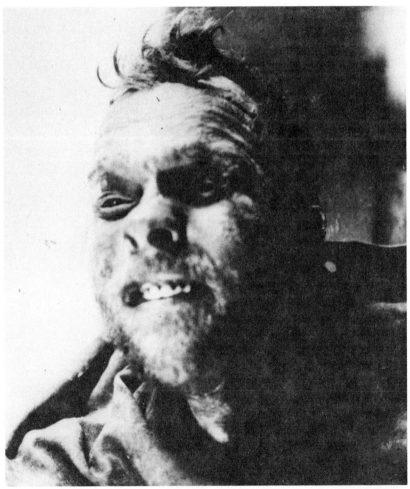

Death photograph of Albert Johnson, 1932. Glenbow Archives, Calgary, Alberta

Empress District of Saskatchewan. "A smart, intelligent fellow able to do forty miles a day through the snow-clad country with little more exertion than one might experience from a Sunday afternoon walk."

The police themselves had no answer and, from the few possessions found on the body of the lone wolf — who had not uttered a single word to his adversaries during the forty-eight day war — they could glean little of his origins or identity. Apart from his snowshoes, canoe, and weapons (which later found their way into the R.C.M.P. museum in Regina), the Mad Trapper left little for posterity: a jar of pearls, a little alluvial gold, a few pieces of gold dental work (not his own). But he did own, as the police discovered, $2,410 in cash: a sum which would have taken the Blueberry Kid on a Tri Star jet, or a Chicago gangster with a fedora near an airport, a lot further than the Eagle River.

6
THE HOUSEBOY

Many years ago, when rum was run and dope peddled, there lived in a big house in Point Grey, British Columbia, a houseboy and a nursemaid. The houseboy was, in the parlance of the times, a "Chinaman," attached, like a crystal chandelier, to the fancy Shaughnessy home, at 3851 Osler Avenue, of the well-connected Mr. R. P. Baker, son-in-law of the lumber tycoon and political notable, General A. D. McRae. The nursemaid, Janet Kennedy Smith, a recent Scottish immigrant, was employed by Mr. Baker's brother, Frederick Lefevre, a Jericho Tennis Club devotee and agent for the drug-importing firms of Baker-Golwynne Company Limited and Stevens-Baker Company.

Wong and Janet's joint residency followed R. P.'s departure with his family for England in the spring of 1924, and the arrival back in Vancouver of brother F. L. some months earlier, following a brief stay in Europe, where, in addition to hiring Janet to care for his infant daughter, he looked after some international business transactions. F. L. took up R. P.'s offer to sit in at Osler Avenue, since the family's Nelson Street house, near Stanley Park downtown, was undergoing renovations. Like the manicured shrubs and Victorian bric-a-brac, Wong Foon Sing came with the house.

Wong and Janet got along well, or so it seemed. Janet earned her twenty dollars a month by tending to the Baker child in the nursery upstairs, fed and bathed the baby, did the washing in the basement laundry room, and helped Wong with special chores like the canning of summer berries. Employed as a launderer and domestic at a succession of places following his immigration to Vancouver in 1914, Wong stuck to his usual routines. He cared for the verandah plants, polished brass and silver, swept up, prepared meals, washed dishes. On the occasion of Janet's 22nd birthday, he presented her, as a show of affection, with a silk nightie and two camisoles.

The morning of Saturday, July 26, 1924, was like most others in the

Baker household. Well rested after a vigorous match in the semifinals at the Lower Mainland Tennis Tournament at Jericho, F. L. rose before eight, breakfasted, and departed with his wife; F. L. heading for his office downtown, and his wife Doreen for their Nelson Street house, the Bank of Montreal, and Spencer's store. Wong and Janet, in the meanwhile, tended to their separate chores. Janet calmed and napped the baby, hung a few garments out to dry, and wandered up and down the stairs with piles of clothes, before settling into some serious ironing in the basement laundry room. So busy was Wong with his polishing, dishwashing, and plant tending that he barely noticed Janet's comings and goings throughout the morning. At noon, however, while peeling potatoes in preparation for lunch, Janet was recalled to Wong's mind by a loud explosion. At first Wong thought that a car had backfired or blown a tire in the street nearby, and he glanced out of the kitchen window to determine the cause. Further consideration, however, sent him running downstairs, into the basement.

On arrival at the laundry room, Wong Foon Sing found Janet Smith, clothed in her blue denim dress and white stockings and shoes, lying motionless on her back, her head under the ironing board and feet pointed towards the laundry tubs opposite. Beside her outstretched right arm was a .45-caliber long-barreled pistol, a war memento which F. L. Baker had stored in a haversack in the hallway upstairs. Nearby lay a hand iron still attached to its socket and warm from recent use. When Wong knelt down and raised the girl's head, he observed a bloody wound in her right temple and a frozen stare in her opened eyes. Wong noted a slight movement of the lips before he laid Janet's head back, wiped his bloody hands on her white apron, and ran upstairs to call Mr. Baker on the telephone.

Informed in broken English that "nursey" was dead, F. L. Baker rushed home and found Janet just as the excited houseboy had described her. When Wong reached for the gun, Baker told him not to touch anything. Baker phoned the Point Grey municipal police and spoke with a Constable James E. Green, who, accompanied by a Dr. Bertie Blackwood, arrived within minutes. Dr. Blackwood pronounced Janet dead, while Constable Green, after some brief snooping, announced it was a clear case of suicide, not dissimilar from some forty others he had seen in his lifetime. On the orders of Coroner W. D. Brydone-Jack, the body was removed by the undertaking firm of John Edwards, embalmed, and readied for the autopsy and coroner's inquest set for Monday, July 28.

The inquest was routine and brief. Mr. Baker, Wong Foon Sing, Dr. Blackwood, Constable Green, and several acquaintances of Janet were all heard, together with a pair of workmen employed on a construction project next door, who testified that they had stopped work at 10:30 in the morning on the Saturday of her death to hear "the Scottish nightingale" singing outside the Bakers' bedroom window. All of this was absorbed by Mr. Brydone-Jack and the jurors who concluded that poor Janet Smith had "come to her death at 3851 Osler Street, Point Grey Municipality, B.C. on July 26th, 1924 as the result of a gunshot wound of the head from a revolver accidentally discharged by herself." Two days later, the memorial and burial services, arranged by Mr. Baker and presided over by Rev. J. S. Henderson, D.D., were held at Saint Andrew's United Church, which the girl had regularly attended. The body was buried in Mountain View Cemetery.

It was all very sad, and straightforward, to Coroner Brydone-Jack, the jurors, the Point Grey police. A lonely lass from the Old Country had taken her own life, by accident or design, thousands of miles from home, at the farthest edge of a cruel new world. But their perfunctory investigation, and the curious procedures employed, raised some questions. Constable Green and his colleagues, it turned out, had handled the fatal gun so many times before examination that no discernable fingerprints remained as evidence of who had held the gun before the police arrived. The fatal bullet and the corresponding mark on the basement wall were not located until several days after the incident, when a Constable F. O. Fish conducted a follow-up investigation. Equally odd was the coroner's directive to the mortician to embalm the body before delivery to the autospy, a procedure that interfered with the inspection of the wound and the determination of whether any criminal or sexual assault had occurred. It was later alleged, as well, that the embalming method itself was unorthodox.

These mysterious irregularities did not go unnoticed by Janet's concerned ethnic kin, and by a press that sniffed the newsworthy potential of a mystery death set appropriately among high hedges, sweeping crescents, and beautiful people. Had Janet collapsed in a workingman's cottage in east Vancouver, on a thirty-three-foot-wide lot bounded by a lime-green picket fence — and in different racial company — she might well have joined the obscure ranks of Constable James Green's forty others. But she, or her murderer, had chosen a more splendid milieu, a big house in Shaughnessy Heights where gentlemen tycoons and their smart ladies — assisted by Oriental houseboys — partied lavishly, pulled at strings, and, it was rumored, conspired against public morality and decent, upright classes. More importantly, the poor white Smith girl had fallen dead in uncomfortable proximity to a mysterious stranger; a "Chinaman," member of a race long reviled in British Columbia and given, it was alleged, to gambling, opium, deceit, lechery, and strange rituals in secret societies.

Headlines in the Vancouver Evening Sun, *September 10, 1924.*

So it was not too long before Janet Smith's death became the Janet Smith Mystery. In the weeks following the inquest, a steady trickle of stories appeared in the *Vancouver Daily Province*, the morning and evening *Sun*, the *Daily Colonist* and *Daily Times* in Victoria, and the *Saturday Weekly Tribune*, hinting at inquest irregularities, diary disclosures, strange parties, and Janet's victimization by "Chinamen." Neighboring nursemaids and old boyfriends were interviewed, and their comments reported about Janet's sunny, cheerful disposition; her hopefulness; and her aversion to the Chinese houseboy. It was reported thirdhand that Wong Foon Sing had touched Janet's hand when he brought her food, an intimacy which inspired loathing in the girl. A mysterious Oriental gardener, who disappeared behind neighboring hedges soon after the incident, was also the subject of press speculation.

Feeding the journalists were the upright gentlemen of the Council of the Scottish Societies, an umbrella committee representing scattered Hibernian groups across the province, which looked after the social needs of immigrant kin. Well placed near the top of the ethnic pecking order, the Scots took up cudgels on behalf of the nightingale, held several open meetings, invited information, formed an investigative committee and hired Mr. Alex Henderson, a prominent attorney, as legal advisor and chief investigator.

The Scottish efforts brought results. After perusing the inquest evidence, conversing with Mr. Henderson, and concluding that the Point Grey police were not Scotland Yard, the attorney general of British Columbia, the Honourable A. M. Manson, appointed a Mr. C. W. Craig, K.C., to examine all aspects of the case and recommend action. In the meanwhile, the provincial police, spearheaded by Inspector Forbes Cruikshank and assisted by a private detective, lent assistance to their Point Grey colleagues in the furtherance of the cause of justice. In the early evening of August 12, Wong Foon Sing was intercepted as he alighted from a tram on Cordova and Carroll streets in Vancouver's Chinatown, shoved into a waiting car, and removed to an office in the Empire Building downtown, where he was roughly interrogated for eight hours, before being released at 5:30 the next morning.

The Honourable Alex M. Manson, K.C., Attorney General and Grand Master, 1925. Provincial Archives of British Columbia

Although Wong Foon Sing told his abductors nothing new, Mr. Craig, in his own investigations, had found enough "irregularities" in the Point Grey investigation to initiate proceedings for a second inquest. An application to the Supreme Court by the attorney general directing the coroner to order the body exhumed was favorably considered, and a panel of six surgeons and an autopsy expert examined the Smith girl's corpse at the Vancouver General Hospital morgue and reported their findings. A hearing was set for Thursday, September 4.

The first inquest into the death of Janet Smith had been an obscure meeting; the second was a large public event. The judge's chambers, the juryroom, the benches of the prisoners' dock, the steps of Coroner Brydone-Jack's dais, the rail of the jurybox, were raided by a platoon of spectators, mostly women, many of whom brought lunches to sustain them through the day-long sessions. For six full days the spectators and jurors heard about bullet valences, modes of collapse of falling bodies, parallel and transverse fractures, mysterious burns on the dead girl's forearm, probable and improbable angles of bullet entries, and the absence of powder burns on the girl's head, which Dr. Hunter thought improbable in the event of her shooting herself, but not impossible. The drug business of Mr. Baker and the movements of him and his wife on the day of Janet's death were probed, together with the desultory investigations of the Point Grey police. The star witness, again, was Wong Foon Sing, whose testimony was preceded by a dispute about whether the "fire" or "chicken" oath should be administered to the quaint Oriental. The court settled for the chicken and took Wong outside where a piece of paper was burnt, with candles and joss sticks, and a chicken killed. When Wong appeared for his second day of testimony, the duration of a chicken oath was debated and the conclusion drawn that it lasted a mere twenty-four hours. So a second chicken was killed.

Poultry sacrifices notwithstanding, Wong Foon Sing repeated essentially the same story he gave at the first inquest. He had barely seen Janet that morning until he heard the loud explosion around noon. On going downstairs, he found her on her back in the laundry room, the revolver and flatiron beside the motionless body. He had seen no one else in the house that morning besides the Bakers, who had left the house around 9:00 A.M. Neither Mr. Craig, representing the attorney general, nor Mr. Henderson, who appeared on behalf of the Scottish Society, could shake his simple story. To confuse matters further, Wong's counsel, Mr. Harry Senkler, read choice extracts from Janet's diary, which had been alluded to in press reports and placed in the possession of the coroner. Janet, it seems, thought well of Wong, appreciated his devotion, his occasional gifts of chocolates, film, and clothing, his willingness to wash her clothes and prepare her food. And there were more than a few entries, which Mr.

Senkler read to a hushed audience, indicating that the "singing nursemaid" was, by her own admission, "terribly flirtatious," subject to depressions, and fond of male companionship. There was Carl, who drove her around in his automobile, strolled with her in the park and protested his love; Arthur, a Robert's Creek resident and ardent admirer, of whom she had tired; "good and steady" John, who wanted to marry her. In addition, Lake, George, Jones, Paul, Norris, Morrison, and a Teddy Forrester made their separate appearances at odd intervals.

The jurors took this all in, and on Wednesday, September 10, foreman James Wilson announced their decision after "one of the most thorough and protracted inquiries of its kind ever held in British Columbia." "We find that Janet K. Smith, was, on July 26th, 1924, wilfully murdered in the course of her employment in the laundry basement of 3851 Osler Avenue by being shot through the head by a revolver, but by whom fired we have no evidence to show." Following the abatement of the prolonged applause by court spectators, Mr. Wilson continued: "the want of any proper investigation when the tragedy was discovered was responsible for this protracted inquiry and caused great suffering to innocent persons and probably shielded guilt . . . it is regrettable that the reading of picked extracts from the deceased's diary tended to defame her pure and unsullied memory."

However besmirched Janet Smith's memory may have become, there was no letup, during the succeeding months, in the spread of rumors, the quarreling among authorities, or in the rate of duplication of investigations — official and unofficial. To prosecute their own search, the Hibernians retained the services of a "famous detective" attached to an agency of "international reputation." Among those sought, the press reported, was the mysterious Chinese gardener, who had allegedly consorted with Wong on the day of the death, before vanishing among the brambles and bushes of Shaughnessy Heights. A search of the Baker home by a team of investigators, it was disclosed, had yielded from the furnace a telltale corset and a man's handkerchief stained with blood, although what eventually became of these prize apparels, remained a mystery. Reports of a vanished party dress, supposedly worn by Janet before the murderer changed her clothes, and of obtuse experiments with flatirons crept into the press.

While rumors multiplied, the authorities sniped. The indignant central ratepayers of Vancouver censured the coroner. Point Grey ratepayers went further and, in early January, 1925, voted in a new police commission, who promptly dismissed Chief of Police Simpson and Constable James Green, who had been placed under suspension by the old commission. "If you want to do murder and get away with it," the insurgents announced, "Point Grey is a good place to go."

In Victoria, Janet Smith's spirit wafted into the very halls of the Legislature where Mrs. Mary Ellen Smith, a women's rights activist, former Liberal minister without portfolio, and first woman to win election to any legislature in Canada, introduced a bill banning the employment of the Chinese alongside white girls in residential homes. The bill was not received kindly by the Chinese consul in Vancouver, Lin Pao Heng, who, at a conference with Premier Oliver, "protested emphatically against the introduction of racial considerations on such slim grounds as the Janet Smith murder case." Fortunately for Wong's fellow domestics, the legislators shared the consul's opposition, although for different reasons. "Opposition to the bill among politicians is based on the fear that its enactment would result only in the dismissal of large numbers of white servant girls," the *Sun* reported; "employers of servants apparently prefer Chinese servants to white women. This is indicated by the fact a large number of white domestics have left Vancouver homes, refusing to work with Orientals. Their employers evidently declined to dismiss their Chinese servants."

Mrs. Smith's bill died, but the search for Miss Smith's murderer struggled on. When the Honourable P. G. Coventry, the Conservative M.L.A. for Saanich and an ex-member of the R.C.M.P., tabled a motion in the Legislature urging the government to call in the force, since the Smith murder was tied up with "the real centre and kernel of the higher-up dope ring in the province," the attorney general defended his own actions and those of the provincial police so vigorously that the member withdrew his motion and congratulated the minister. Manson reminded the House that there had never been a lull in "the ceaseless search of the provincial police to get at the facts," noted that "the field of investigation" was circumscribed by a "very narrow circle," and, in a grand final assurance, informed his colleagues that "only recently a young man with some talent in criminal investigation" had been engaged to study the facts and "see if he could not construct some theory that would lead to results."

Mr. Manson's new secret weapon was a Victoria lawyer, Mr. M. B. Jackson, a former member of the Legislature for the Island, Liberal activist, and King's Counsel, who brought a certain energy and verve to the task of theory construction. In the weeks and months following his appointment, he poured over evidence of the hearings, sifted through autopsy reports, read police files, and sailed manfully back and forth between island and mainland collecting new and startling data. While Mr. Jackson sniffed and sailed, scattering newsworthy releases in his wake, the press, Island and mainland, warmed to the cause and hinted at imminent arrests and final solutions. In furtherance of his research, Jackson visited a Victoria slaughterhouse, pumped rounds of bullets into pigs' and cows' heads, then passed on to the morgue of the Essondale Asylum, where the unclaimed corpse of a deceased lunatic was released by the superintendent of mental hospitals, on request of the attorney general and deputy provincial secretary, for scientific experimentation. As the dead lunatic lay flat on his back, oblivious to the purpose of science, Mr. Jackson, accompanied by Inspector Forbes Cruikshank and Dr. A. W. Hunter, the autopsy specialist, stole up and blasted, at a distance of four inches, a .45-caliber bullet into its demented brain. The scattering of the tissue, the resultant parallel as opposed to transverse fracture of the skull, the odd upward trajectory of the emergent bullet, the flattening of its nose, apparently proved profoundly significant. "The bullet was absolutely flattened out," the attorney general later exclaimed to the House in a ringing defense of the Essondale assault, "instead of being only slightly deflected. But there was something else, the bullet ricocheted, struck the ceiling and instead of doing what the bullet in the basement did, it followed the old rule of the angle of resistance and deflection, and went to the floor where it should have landed. The bullet in the Janet Smith case absolutely disobeyed the law of physics."

Incensed at Mr. Jackson's necromaniacal doings, Mr. H. D. Twigg, a Conservative member for Victoria, introduced a resolution in the Legislature calling for an investigation by a select committee of the House. It was Twigg's view that since the provincial secretary had charge of lunatic asylums and the attorney general of British Columbia was "by law," if not in fact, "a committee of lunacy," they were "each guilty of dereliction of duty in the discharge of their respective functions, and that they had aroused a general feeling of distrust, disapprobation and horror of them throughout the province by their respective actions in acquiescing in and allowing the use of human remains for unlawful purposes."

Twigg's barbs carried little weight. Hot on the trail of the dark assassins loose somewhere among the great boughs and silent mansions of Shaughnessy Heights, Jackson persisted, during the winter months of 1924 and 1925, with his dogged sailings, his violent shifting of the facts, and theoretical constructions. In his wanderings through Mr. Manson's "narrowly circumscribed field of investigation," the Victoria special investigator rubbed shoulders and bumped elbows with hordes of other sleuths — provincial policemen, Scottish counselors, ratepayers, Point Grey commissioners, Greater Vancouver policemen, clairvoyants, and private detectives. Among them was a fiftyish private investigator, specializing in liquor and drug matters, and obsessed with the notion that true knowledge of events surrounding the Smith murder lay buried in only one place — the inscrutable brain of the Chinese houseboy.

Now Oscar Beverley Vivian Robinson, O.B.V. for short, was not a reticent sort. Twenty-five years in the snooping business, boss of the Canadian Detective Bureau with the offices in the Empire Building downtown, and descendent, it was said, "of one of the most historic families in the history of Upper Canada," Robinson was an early participant in the Janet Smith mystery play. When Wong was first abducted from Chinatown in August, 1924, by a team of police and private investigators including the police agent Wong Foon Sien, it was to O. B. V. Robinson's office in the Empire Building that the houseboy was removed, where he was interrogated and beaten before his committal to the police station and return to the Baker home. Although Wong disclosed very little, Robinson remained convinced that it was only because the interview had been too short and not thorough enough.

O. B. V. Robinson, in short, wanted a second shot at the houseboy and, in the weeks following the Carroll Street abduction, spared no effort in taking his case before the authorities. The subject was broached in August at a meeting at Mr. Robinson's house, attended by Alex Henderson and by Inspector Owen and Superintendent McMullen of the provincial police. A month later, Mr. Robinson landed in Victoria with a letter of introduction to the premier from his lawyer-son Joseph Oliver in his pocket, and met again with Colonel McMullen, who, in turn, arranged an interview with the attorney general at which, Robinson reported, "secret service work" relating to narcotics and liquor administration as well as to the Janet Smith case was discussed. The attorney general was approached on the same subject a second time at the Court House in downtown Vancouver where, according to Manson, a proposal to abduct Wong was rejected as un-Canadian. "Man, do you understand you are in Canada?" Manson recounted, "we can't do such things here." There were several meetings as well during the winter months, between Robinson and M. B. Jackson, at which an abduction scheme and the employment of Robinson as a special investigator were broached.

In his quest for employment as a special investigator, Robinson received a sympathetic hearing from the Point Grey authorities. In March, the Point Grey officials authorized his hiring as a special investigator at a salary of $300 per month. Later, cheques totalling over $1,270 were advanced on authority of Reeve J. A. Paton out of the contingency fund to Chief John Murdock, who passed on the money to O. B. V. Robinson.

At last funded, Robinson finalized the Wong Foon Sing abduction scheme in early March, 1925. Using the pseudonym of Mr. Hendricks, he approached a real-estate agency, and for $47 a month, rented a small house in a quiet residential neighborhood, situated a few short minutes by car from the fringes of Shaughnessy Heights. As aides and assistants, he engaged his seventeen-year-old son, William, at $5 a day and an unemployed former employee, Mr. Verity W. Norton, who was promised $7.50 a day, $800 minimum, a job with the liquor control board and, finally, immunity from prosecution, based upon assurances received, according to Robinson, from M. B. Jackson and the attorney general himself.

In the early evening of March 20, four hooded men, dressed in flowing white gowns and seated in a baby Grand Chevrolet, drove up and parked a short distance from the residence of Mr. R. P. Baker, who was absent with his wife at the Jericho Club. Leaving a Mr. Wrightson, a building contractor and friend of Robinson, at the wheel and son Willie outside as a guard, O. B. V. and Verity walked to the front door, rang the doorbell and, on receiving no response, entered with a pass key. After lurking briefly in the hallway, they descended into the basement where, with the aid of some heavy equipment and a flashlight, the door was removed from Mr. Wong Foon Sing's sleeping room. Wong was not there, it turned out, and had left only moments earlier, through the basement door, for an evening with friends in Chinatown. On reaching the street outside, however, Wong noticed several mysterious strangers lurking about, so he returned home to the basement. Here he was greeted by O. B. V. and Verity who struck him; threw him to the ground; fitted him with handcuffs, leg chains, blindfold, and gag; and removed him to the car in front. "I pull back and cry out," Wong later recounted. "I yell 'murder,' 'help' and scream loud as I can. Nobody come and men push me and lift me in automobile. I still scream and they hit me and slap me and tell me keep quiet. Then one strike me hard on head, I feel my head very sore and buzz."

Wong Foon Sing was driven around awhile, told of a border crossing into the United States, then removed to the quiet little home of Mr. Hendricks. Here his ordeal began. "They first slapped me with their hands, and then struck with their feet," he recalled; "then they bumped my head against the wall. My left eye was black for a month. After they hit me I could not see with that eye. They hit me on the nose and blood came. Then they washed me up. Two days after they struck me again and this time one said 'Kill the _____ , and we'll get $10,000.' Then they washed my face and gave me water. Two days after they struck me the same way again."

So it went, for days and weeks. Between interrogations, Wong lay on a bed chained to the floor, in a room with the windows boarded up and covered with muslin. He was fed three times a day, on a diet of canned goods primarily and allowed to relieve himself twice a day in the company of armed guards. After nearly every meal he felt sick and vomited. On two or three separate occasions, he was removed to an adjoining room and photographed against the backdrop of a white sheet.

137

on which a picture of a body hanging from a noose and the word
"Justice" were inscribed. The backdrop for another photographic session
consisted of photos of Janet Smith against the white sheet. Otherwise, his
interrogators, dressed in white robes and long pointed hats, with slits at
the eyes and mouth, their hands covered with gloves, continued their
relentless questioning. They held guns to his head, threatened and beat
him, showed him pictures of his wife in China whom, it was promised, he
would never see again. After countless sessions, he was dragged upstairs
into an attic and told his end was near. There before him, hanging from
the rafters, were a rope and noose and, below, a raised platform. "They
put me on chair," he recalled, "and fixed rope on my head. Man says you
tell everything or we kill you. You tell or you be dead. I say I no can tell
any more. I know nothing more about poor nursey. Man say again they
hang me. Men pull chair and I feel rope . . . then I die. . . . When I wake
up I lying on floor. Man is beside me and I think he doctor. He felt my
hand and put his hand on my side. I hear doctor speak to other man. He
say him very near dead. He say not hurt him more, perhaps he die. I very
sick and my clothes all dirty. I feel like going to die. They take me down
to room and put chain on me. Put chain on feet and tie chain around me.
I not stand, I fall on floor. I lie on floor for long time. I very sick for long
time, plenty days."

While this cosy little drama was enacted in a small bungalow on the
fringes of Shaughnessy Heights, where neighbors surmised that a poor
invalid was being mercifully nursed, the world outside wondered what
ever happened to Wong Foon Sing. The abduction, headlined in the
Province, "White Robes Carry China Boy Away," invited an orgy of
speculation, fantasizing, and, in local Chinese circles, concern. In the
days and weeks following his disappearance, it was variously rumored
that he had been secreted, by persons and for reasons unknown, to the
United States, to Mexico, or to Stuart Island in the Gulf of Georgia. He
was located among Chinese lepers; among dope peddlars and rum-run-
ners near Port Kells, less than a dozen miles from New Westminster; at
the home of von MacKensen, a German who had been held in custody
during the war. The press speculated about his residency in a "cave-like
refuge" where in the early war years, German arms had been stored, "an
ideal hiding place carefully chosen in the days when the Kaiser planned
his great coup and had his chosen lieutenants here in readiness for 'Der
Tag.' " One school of thought maintained that Wong's own people, the
Chinese, had shipped him home, on a slow boat.

The local Chinese, understandably, were not parties to this theory.
While the Scottish societies lapsed into a strange silence, the Chinese
rushed into action. At meetings in Chinatown, funds were voted and a
committee struck to investigate the case and pressure the authorities.

Telegrams were sent off to the federal Department of Justice and the provincial attorney general. Soon after Wong's disappearance, the Chinese consul visited the Baker residence and, after noting the broken door, the signs of struggle in Wong's room, the strange inability of the housemaid upstairs — she subsequently disappeared — to hear any noises at the time of the abduction, Wong's impecunious state before departure, and his failure to contact close relatives, concluded that the houseboy had definitely been abducted. A $500 reward was offered for information leading to the capture of the abductors, later increased to $3,000.

Curiously enough, the provincial government did not see fit to offer any inducements of its own. According to Mr. Manson, the news of Wong's removal arrived at an awkward moment — in the midst of a game of golf at Victoria's Upland Links. The bearer of the message was Mr. Jackson, who drove his car next to a hole in the fairway fence, crawled through, and announced his theory that Wong was likely aboard the *Empress of Australia,* steaming towards the Orient on his own volition. The attorney general set aside his tee, approach, or putt shots long enough to consider Mr. Jackson's suggestion that an airplane carrying police officers who knew Wong be sent after the ship, land on the ocean nearby, and return the houseboy. This plan was later abandoned, however, on the advice of the C.P.R. weather bureau, which advised that the seas were choppy. Instead a wire was reputedly sent, with Wong's description, and a reply received that no such person was on board.

With the *Empress* at sea, the attorney general entertained other notions. He brooded darkly over the Canadian branch of the Ku Klux Klan, which, at the instigation of a Mr. Luther Powell in Portland, Oregon, had infiltrated into Vancouver and located at a fancy Shaughnessy address, bringing with it an entire panoply of grand kliegels, beagles, pointed hoods, and flowing gowns. While the Klansmen were otherwise rigid types, they proved flexible, even tolerant, when it came to choosing scapegoats. While blacks were accepted — indeed, favored — as goats in the American South, in the Pacific Northwest, where pralines and grits were as scarce as rhythmic bodies, red melons, and flashing white teeth, the Orientals sufficed. A confirmed Liberal and Canadian, whose penchant for secret societies did not extend beyond the Masonic Grand Lodge, Manson was troubled by the Klan, followed its activities, and alluded to a secret report in a special file outlining a plan to kidnap Wong, himself, Mr. J. H. Senkler, and F. L. Baker.[1]

---

1. Not all of British Columbia's legislators shared Manson's dislikes. During a debate on the admissibility of the Klan into British Columbia, a member declared that if the Klan was against Catholics, Jews, and Negroes, there was no place for it in the British Columbia community, but "if it freed the province of Orientals, he would be for it."

What disturbed Manson and Jackson even more, it turned out, was the fumbling hand in the Wong affair of O. B. V. Robinson, who, in submission to continental taste preferences, passed over McGregor kilts and McDonald tartans in his choice of kidnapping regalia. Although he himself may not have been privy to the abduction at the outset, Manson had good reason, very early, to suspect O. B. V. The private detective had participated in one abduction already, sanctioned by the provincial police, and had talked loudly about a second one to the attorney general himself, to Mr. Jackson, provincial police, the Scottish society, the Point Grey commissioners, and everyone else within earshot. Whatever the prior state of his knowledge, Manson's suspicions must have sharpened somewhat when his special investigator dropped by with photographs of an unhappy Chinese sitting glumly in front of a backdrop adorned with a picture of a young girl. It was Wong Foon Sing.

Jackson, it seems, received the photo from Robinson as proof of his own "subterranean" knowledge of the whereabouts of Wong Foon Sing. Since Wong was nearby somewhere, alive, captive, and under stress, Jackson decided to seize the opportunity — not to arrest Robinson and bare the plot, heaven forbid, but to extract a statement or confession from Robinson's illegally detained prisoner. In pursuit of this end, Jackson arranged a special meeting in the office of the Chinese consul, which was attended by Mr. J. H. Senkler and arranged by Wong's brother, Wong Gow. There it was proposed that a letter be drawn up, authenticated with the consular seal and signed by the consul and Wong's relatives, inviting Wong to tell all he knew in return for a guarantee of freedom from prosecution in the event of his innocence. The courier, it was proposed, would be a journalist privy to Wong's incarceration, a Mr. John Sedgewick Cowper.

Cowper was quite willing to help out. A former Liberal member of the Legislature, proprietor and publisher of a local scandal sheet, the *Saturday Tribune*, he nourished an array of prejudices fitting to the Janet Smith mystery. To begin with, Cowper loathed Orientals and had made himself, over the years, an expert on rising tides, though not of the marine sort. In 1921, for example, while employed by the *Vancouver Daily World*, he had traveled the length and breadth of the province ferreting out yellow perils, for a series of twenty articles titled "The Rising Tide of Asiatics in B.C." But Cowper's hates were not confined to Orientals. They overflowed to include the metro dailies, especially the *Vancouver Daily Province*, which had fired him; the Vancouver police; the Liberal party; the Conservative party; and traffickers in drugs and alcohol linked up through mysterious conduits to high centers of power. A social purist and subscriber to the Sino-Shaughnessy conspiracy theory, Cowper found in the Janet Smith mystery, a perfect means of venting his pet hates, flogging the local establishment, and boosting his paper's meager circulation.

When Robinson first approached Cowper about Wong's disappearance, the *Tribune* editor knew he had a good story. He slipped Robinson $50 as a retainer for a confession exclusive and, draped in Klan robes and posing as a doctor, visited Wong and took his picture. The photo was then reproduced in the *Tribune* with a request for contributions to the Wong Foon Sing Sustenance Fund. Cowper collected $54.70 and passed the money on to Robinson for canned sardines, Klik, Spam, and other diarrheic stimulants.

Eager for a bigger scoop, Cowper was agreeable to the suggestion that he transmit Jackson's offer to Wong. The spoiler, it turned out, was Mr. Senkler who, aside from placing little faith in Cowper's veracity, understandably questioned the utility and ethics of obtaining a statement, confession, admission, disclaimer, or whatever, from an illegally detained prisoner. So he refused Jackson's suggestion, washed his hands of the project, and filed away a record of the meeting.

By late April, it appeared, Wong's captors were prepared for some disengagements of their own. By prolonging his detention, Robinson and company risked embarrassing disclosures by a press frantically beating the woods nearby. Besides, there were funding problems and pressures from above. Neither Point Grey nor Victoria, whatever the extent of its complicity, was ready to finance or countenance an extended imprisonment. And, it turned out, both had special plans for Mr. Wong upon release. On April 29, the Point Grey commissioners met in H. P. McCraney's office, heard a report from Robinson about his investigations into the Janet Smith case, and dispatched an envoy, in the person of an H. O. MacDonald, to consult with Mr. Jackson and the attorney general in Victoria.

Wong felt the results of this meeting in the early morning hours of May 1, when he was awakened in his cell, slapped about, dressed, shackled and blindfolded, removed to an adjoining room, and then taken to a waiting car. In the company of Verity Norton, and Sergeant Neil MacPherson and Constable William Munro of the Point Grey police force, who had been sent on instruction of Chief John Murdock, he was driven around awhile before learning from his companions that the international border between the state of Washington and the province of British Columbia had finally been crossed. Within an hour, the car stopped and Wong was led into a clump of bushes at the corner of Angus Avenue and Marine Drive, not far from Mr. Hendrick's house, where Verity Norton quickly disappeared. Within seconds, a policeman approached him with the question, "What are you doing here?" removed his blindfold and led him into the back seat of a waiting car. The police then drove Wong to a small building nearby, the Marpole police substation, where the confused houseboy, with aching head and buzzing ear, was charged with the murder of Janet Smith. The headline the next day read, "Houseboy Thrown from Motorcar on Marine Drive."

Wong's odd removal from Mr. Hendrick's nursing home to Oakalla Prison — via the Marine Drive bushes and Point Grey police substation — was not kindly received by the Chinese or their sympathetic friends. In the days following Wong's Oakalla committal, questions were asked and remained unanswered. Questions about the mysterious person who had told the police of the queer boy wandering in the bushes at 3 A.M.; about the failure of the same anonymous caller to claim the reward offered by the Chinese; about Victoria's failure to post a reward; about Wong's location in captivity and the identity of his captors, which people like John Sedgewick Cowper obviously knew something about; about the extent of Point Grey and Victoria's knowledge and complicity in the entire affair. "Ever since the death of Janet Smith, the young China boy has been persecuted," the *Sun* editorialized. "He was kidnapped by police officers and given the third degree. Then he was abducted by some unknown agency and held for 42 days, long before any charge had been laid against him. If that had happened to a young Canadian boy in China, a British gunboat would have been on the job in 24 hours." Mass meetings of the Chinese Benevolent Society and the Wong Association, an extended family group to which Wong Foon Sing belonged, passed resolutions demanding official inquiries, setting up a defense fund, and raising the reward offered for information leading to the arrest of the abductors to $3,000. The new Chinese consul general, Mr. Han Chow Kwok, following a briefing from the departing Lin Pao Hang, demanded a royal commission and observed that the reputation of the police system of British Columbia was at stake. His feelings were shared by the Vancouver barristers, who, at their annual meeting, condemned the "illegal, unwarranted and cowardly kidnapping or abduction of Wong Foon Sing" and registered their opposition to "lynch law, mob law, secret society rule, Ku Klux Klan or third degree methods of any kind." The attorney general was "urged to spare neither effort nor expense in tracking down and bringing to justice those guilty of participation in this outrage against the peace, order and good name of British Columbia."

Others, however, were more forward looking and inclined to the view that the abduction was, after all, a red herring and past history, best forgotten. "We are glad that direct action has been taken at last," Mr. David Patterson, president of the Council of the United Scottish Societies, announced, summing up the views of his constituents. "This is a step which I have had reason to anticipate for about a month and it certainly meets with the approval of all our people." Since Wong stood accused, the Scots concluded, then new and startling evidence must have come to light during his detention. The Scots were joined by other upright citizens, panting for results and "blindly and bitterly," as the *Sun* observed, convinced of a conspiracy and Wong's guilt. Nor was interest limited to British Columbia. "The whole story of the murder and subsequent investigation," the *Province* announced on the day of Wong's return, "is one that has already attracted international attention, and it is common knowledge that Scotland Yard detectives are working on one angle of the case, which, it is said, stretches its web right across the continent and to London. It is expected that if the full story is told, it will involve a number of more or less prominent persons."

The man who held the key to the mystery, the insiders all knew, was M. B. Jackson, whose six-month odyssey back and forth from Victoria to Vancouver, had finally brought results. "In his pursuit of the case, Mr. Jackson is understood to have employed both police and unofficial channels," the *Sun* reported, "and it is believed that he kept the strings of the inquiry so close in his own hands that none of the various agencies employed hardly knew the objectives towards which they were being directed, and that the right hand of Mr. Jackson was kept in ignorance of what the left hand was doing."

As it turned out, Jackson really had very little to show, with either hand, at the preliminary hearing, before Magistrate George R. McQueen in the Point Grey Courthouse, where the old evidence, spiced with new histrionics, was rehashed for several days. As nervous as ever, Wong repeated the same story he had told at the first inquest, the second inquest, and, doubtless, during the first abduction and the second abduction. After hearing out and examining the doctors, morticians, bakers, embalmers, and police, Mr. Senkler repeated that there was no evidence that a murder had been committed, or that his client was connected in any way with the girl's death. And after discovering the body, Senkler maintained, Wong had "done everything that an innocent man might be expected to do."

Mr. Jackson, on the other hand, sniffed a conspiracy and filled the court with grand allusions and dramatic non-discoveries. He browbeat witnesses, waved pistols in the air, wondered aloud about the £40,000 of drugs contracted in France and Japan that Mr. Baker insisted on the witness stand were legitimate, under government permit, like all of his other business, and had nothing to do with either Wong or Janet Smith. The shocking revelation that Janet had died with a black mark on her left index finger, a certain indication of cocaine, lost some of its effect when the opinion was offered that brass polish produced a similar effect. Target shooting, with cotton matting, pigs' heads, demented Essondale lunatic brains, bulked large in Jackson's questioning, as did obtuse considerations of angles of blood spattering, modes of collapse, misshapen bullet heads, the imprints of flatirons on human skin and wooden boards. Mr. Jackson closed with a revelation that the basement scene had been "staged to represent a tragedy — in case of accident or otherwise." It was an "inescapable conclusion," he avowed, that "the girl was not killed in that room by that bullet at that time."

That Wong was only remotely — if at all — connected with Mr. Jackson's hypothetical staged murder did not impress Magistrate McQueen. On considering the piles of scanty evidence, which ran to five hundred printed pages, the magistrate committed Wong Foon Sing to stand trial for the murder of Janet Smith at the next court of competent jurisdiction, in October or November. Incensed at the ruling, Senkler launched a habeas corpus action in the Supreme Court where Chief Justice Hunter agreed that the evidence was scanty and unlikely to result in a conviction before a jury, but ruled against the application on grounds of incompetent jurisdiction. The judge invited a bail application instead, and, on June 24, granted Wong Foon Sing a temporary and conditional freedom, on assurance of $10,000 posted in two or more securities.

Wong's release pending trial was welcomed by his friends, supporters, and family. But it in no way stayed the flow of slander, rumors, or court action. Dragged through a spate of criminal hearings, Mr. F. L. Baker decided to initiate an action of his own in the civil courts, against a young society lady who was inclined to jabber. The object of Mr. Baker's wrath was a Miss Monica Mason Rooke, a graduate of Crofton House, "one of the popular girls of the younger set," and daughter of "a highly respected English family." Like other young ladies of the smart set, Miss Rooke wallowed and luxuriated in Janet Smith's affairs and one day in March was heard to whisper, "Isn't it too bad that the Bakers had the party the night before. . . . Oh yes, there was a party. I know two chaps who were there." This was enough for Mr. Baker and his wife who, after consulting a lawyer, launched an action for slander that was subsequently settled out of court.

A Mrs. Dora Bates, whom everybody sought and nobody could find, had equally suggestive opinions about Janet Smith's affairs. A contributor to the internationalization of the Shaughnessy mystery, Mrs. Bates published in the May 17 edition of *The People*, a London, England scandal sheet, her theory that "Janet Smith was the victim of one of the terrible Chinese secret societies that have sprung up in Canada, and the United States." "Like many other poor girls of the western race," Mrs. Bates went on, "she had fallen under the fatal spell of the East and had made friends with Chinamen, who seemed to exercise a terrible fascination over her. . . . One in particular persisted in seeking her out and two nights before the tragedy she came to me in terrible distress of mind saying that she had been threatened with denunciation to some of the secret societies in which the Chinese belonged for breaking faith with this man. . . . We have had in different parts of Canada many unfortunate illustrations of what follows the association of western girls with easterners, whether they be Chinese, Japanese or Indian, and the feeling that Janet had been a victim of another manifestation of eastern interest in western girls has moved our people and stirred up passions that had perhaps been better left undisturbed. It will be brought out in the case that there is in existence a Chinese secret society that makes it its special mission to exert pressure on western girls to force them into marriage with the Chinese . . . and this sinister aspect of the case should not be overlooked by those who try to understand why it is becoming such an important case in Canada."

Although *The People* carried a photo of Mrs. Dora Bates, or of someone from an old album who was supposed to be her, Police Inspector Forbes Cruikshank and his colleagues had no luck in locating the mysterious authoress. Barbara Orford, however, caused no such problem. Unmarried, in her mid-thirties, daughter of a retired British Army Colonel, and an employee of a downtown department store, Miss Orford posed as a seeress, blessed with a "second sight" and an inner knowledge of the true facts of the Janet Smith case. She had first befriended the late maid, or so she claimed, in a public tearoom and was drawn to her Scottish accent, Scottish laughter, and her interest — perhaps Scottish as well — in teacup reading. When Janet died, Miss Orford was distressed and suspicious and attended seances and meetings of the Scottish societies. Being the seventh daughter of a seventh daughter, she was, naturally, clairvoyant and came to know in her mind the true circumstances of her friend's death: the wild party at the Bakers', the sinister dope trade, the maiden's corruption by Orientals and tycoons, mysterious brawls in remote attic rooms, the telling blow with an electric heater kept in the nursery to warm the baby's bottle.

A generous and public-spirited sort, Miss Orford did not keep things to herself and offered her services as seeress to the Scots, the journalists, the police, and Mr. M. B. Jackson, who took copious notes during a lengthy interview. She badgered the Bakers, the McRaes, and the police, to gain admission to the Baker house in order to confirm, test — or modify, if necessary — her second, third, or fourth sights. In the April 26 edition of the *Glasgow Sunday Mail*, Miss Orford, like Mrs. Bates — perhaps the same person — turned authoress and wrote an article entitled "The Murder of Janet Smith: My theory as seen by me identically in three dreams on three successive nights." In it, the usual panoply floated by: drugs, a debauchery, a brawl, tycoons, Chinese, a blow on the head. Unfortunately, the dream faded at a critical moment, on all three nights: "After that I see no more. But the next day I dream exactly the same dream and again on the following night, but all in vain. It had been my hope that I would see something further — something that would show me what happened after the girl was struck on the head." Or by whom.

Now dreams are dreams; and facts, facts. Miss Orford, unfortunately, came to confuse the two. After months of brooding, dreams and facts merged, dialectically and synthetically, into a new form of human knowledge, "dream-facts." Whether the facts preceded the dreams, or vice versa, was not certain, but Miss Orford was excited enough by her revelations to tell all at an interview attended by her lawyer, a Mr. Hamilton Read, Mr. Senkler, and a court stenographer. A full fifty-six pages of free-floating dream-facts was recorded, focusing on a fantastic conspiracy and culminating in a party she now claimed to have attended. "When I was giving the ... confession," she recalled half-laughing, "the words just seemed to be drawn out of me and on to the paper by a magnet. I don't know if anyone stuck a needle into me or not, but that's how it was."

Miss Orford's dream-facts might have died right there had not a fellow subscriber to the Sino-Shaughnessy theory, John Sedgewick Cowper, picked up and broadcast her story. Cowper first met Miss Orford at a Scottish society meeting where he heard of her dreams and sights and things. Intrigued by the investigative potentials of clairvoyance, he communicated with a seer in England, a Mr. Tyler, who, apparently, had helped solve an important crime. Cowper felt that Miss Orford could do the same, if only given a chance. To test her powers, he prevailed upon a fellow journalist to hire a team of private detectives to visit the Baker home. While the maid was entertained by one gentleman in the kitchen downstairs, a colleague slipped upstairs to the nursery, lifted up the rug at Miss Orford's designated place and there discovered, or so Cowper later disclosed, a telltale stain on the wooden floor, resembling blood. The wood chip was removed and presented for examination, according to Mr. Cowper, to City Analyst Vance, whose conclusion was inconclusive.

Cowper, in any event, believed what he wanted to and when informed of Barbara Orford's marathon blurt, he rushed to print it, in modified and outline form. Without naming names, the June 6 edition of the *Saturday Tribune* carried a spirited rehash of the Sino-Shaughnessy conspiracy theory, under the headline "Alleged Eye Witness Confesses in Janet Smith's Murder." The old ingredients were there, without names: a Shaughnessy orgy; drugs and booze; tycoons, politicians, and Orientals; Janet Smith gliding about with glazed eyes serving drinks; her killing at 2:30 A.M.; a hurried burial; a suicide cover-up.

Among the readers of Mr. Cowper's *Tribune* feature was the attorney general, who remained sceptical. "Under certain circumstances, there might be reason for getting excited about the story," Mr. Manson said, "but under the circumstances that exist, I'm not getting excited." Manson did, however, appoint several police officers to check out Orford's facts "with most exceeding care" and appointed an alienist, Dr. G. S. Curtis, to sit in on an interview with her "for the purpose of estimating her mentality." The investigation proved conclusively, according to Manson, that "there was no foundation in fact for her remarkable recital." "She placed a bristling moustache on a man who had been clean shaven for years," the *Province* offered, "and in other cases she made tall men short and stout and declared the short ones were tall and thin." When His Honour the Lieutenant Governor Walter C. Nichol subsequently discovered that his son Jack, General A. D. McRae, Constable James Green, and himself had figured in Miss Orford's dream-facts as guests at the fatal party, he dispensed with the usual Lieutenant-Governor generalities — "The use of my name in the so-called 'confession' made by Barbara Orford, whoever she may be, is not only a gratuitous impertinence, but an unqualified falsehood." As to the alienist's report, it was never made public.

The Bakers' objection, however, did obtain a public airing at the trial of J. S. Cowper. Troubled by the publication of "a summary" of Miss Orford's confession, they sued Cowper for defamatory libel. During the two-day trial in early October, there was much excitement and speculation about whether Miss Orford would appear and, if so, what the likely effect of her testimony would be on Mr. Cowper's fate, the rules of evidence, and phenomenology. Miss Orford, it seemed, had difficulty deciding whether to stick around for the ordeal. "There are two voices calling to me in my head," she confessed; "one says 'fly,' 'go away!' 'disappear.' The other says 'stay,' 'fight.' Tell the world the truth. That voice is the spirit of Janet Smith, coming back to me from the grave." As it turned out, she ignored Janet's pleas and disappeared during Cowper's trial, which ended in a guilty verdict and a sentence of a $200 fine or six months.

Cowper's tribulations did not end there. In mid-June an unfortunate event occurred that affected all of Wong Foon Sing's abductors and detainers. Upset about false promises and monies owing, Verity W. Norton chose to sing, like a Shaughnessy nightingale, or Burnaby pigeon. The result was a flurry of sensational arrests, charges of kidnapping, assault, illegal detention and confinement, and a string of hearings and trials that filled the front pages from mid-June until late November. In the flood of publicity about the kidnapping and about the strange ways in which justice was administered in British Columbia, the ancient mystery of the death of a Scottish nursemaid was quietly forgotten, except among her kin, who remained faithful to her memory. At the beck of the Council of Scottish Societies and in the midst of the spate of preliminary hearings, more than a hundred Scottish people com- memorated, on June 24, the twenty-third anniversary of Janet Smith's birth, with a memorial service at her graveside at Section 1919, Mountain View Cemetery. Bouquets of fresh flowers were laid, together with a pair of wax wreaths, one from her parents — who contributed a one pound note — the other from the Council of Scottish Societies, who inscribed theirs with the words, "In loving memory of Janet Kennedy Smith, who met her death while in the bloom of youth. ...." In a moving speech, David Patterson, the Society's president, referred to Janet Smith as "the little girl ... murdered in Shaughnessy Heights," and noted that "owing to the inaction of the police authorities, the Scottish Societies had been forced to take action in the matter." Rev. Duncan MacDougall, who offered prayers, described Janet as a dutiful daughter who had caused her parents no regrets, likened the judicial system in British Columbia to Turkey's, and expressed his conviction that "there is some man, perhaps there are more than one in this province today, that have upon them the mark of Cain." To be summoned to court in connection with Wong Foon Sing's kidnapping, the Reverend concluded, "was an honour."

There were many who shared it: O. B. V. Robinson and his son William; J. S. Cowper; M. B. Jackson; Point Grey Commissioners H. O. MacDonald and H. P. McCraney; Chief of Police John Murdock and Sgt. Percy Kirkham; Mr. Patterson and Mrs. F. H. Stratton, president and secretary, respectively, of the Council of Scottish Societies, which diverted monies from the Janet Smith investigation fund to cover legal expenses and sponsor a benefit concert at the Saint Andrew and Caledonian Society for the Scots implicated in the abduction.

The star performers in court, were O. B. V. Robinson and Verity Norton. Both admitted and detailed their parts in the abduction and detention, and both freely implicated their superiors. Norton claimed that Robinson had assured him that there would be no prosecutions. The attorney general, M. B. Jackson, the Point Grey and Scottish people, funded and consented to the operation. He claimed that David Patterson and Mrs. Stratton had been lurking outside the Baker home when he arrived to abduct Wong and that Commissioner H. O. MacDonald and the Point Grey Police Chief J. Murdock had visited and interrogated Wong in detention. It had been Murdock and Kirkham, Robinson insisted, who supplied the guns and handcuffs used in the abduction and the same officers who had assisted in the removal of Wong to the Marine Drive bushes precedent to his pickup and transfer to the police station.

Robinson spared nobody, from the attorney general down, in his own testimony, corroborated by his secretary Mrs. Elizabeth Donnelly. Manson, he insisted, had suggested a kidnapping during one of their meetings. Jackson had agreed to it during a winter meeting, in January or February; had met with him numerous times to discuss detention matters; and had given him repeated assurances of immunity. The Point Grey commissioners, who had employed him as a special investigator, had known about and agreed to his actions from the outset. Money, from a contingency fund used to sustain Wong, had been passed on to him on several occasions by Chief Murdock who, with Sergeant Kirkham, had supplied guns and handcuffs before the abduction. Robinson insisted that the first abduction of Wong, in August, 1924, had had the support of the Victoria authorities; it had been reasonable to assume that the second abduction also met with their approval.

The juror had no problem with the Robinsons and Norton. They were found guilty after brief deliberations, but strong recommendations of mercy were entered, likely in the belief that some support, consent, or tolerance had come from above. O. B. V. was given a year in prison, Norton nine months. Willie Robinson received a suspended sentence.

The Point Grey people — MacDonald, Murdock, and Kirkham — fared better at their trials, which heard Messrs. Manson and Jackson protest their own innocence. None denied that Robinson had been employed and funded by them as a special investigator to look into the Janet Smith matter. But they denied any role in the abduction or detention. It was not until late April that they had learned about what Robinson had done, or where Wong was kept. After that, full efforts had been made to effect Wong's release.

The jurors bought their story and acquitted all three. Convinced that sufficient justice had already been done, Manson decided to clear the court by entering a stay of proceedings in the cases of M. B. Jackson and the remaining Point Grey commissioners and Scottish Society councillors.[2] When the House heard of the reasons for the use of the procedure of nolle prosequi, the Liberals cheered, Conservatives jeered, and Mr. Tom Uphill, the Labour member for Fernie, enquired, "Who is this girl Nellie Pros? I never heard of her."

Mr. Manson had, and she proved helpful in bumping Janet Smith from the court rolls and front pages of an incensed press. The attorney general had his own theories and regrets about the entire affair. "I would, with all my heart that these pages in our history had not been written," he confided to the House, "Pages that have their origin, after all, in what? In the spleen, the clever diabolical mind of a man of no morals, who through a slimy sheet had broadcast to the world increasingly, for almost

---

2. J. S. Cowper was acquitted.

18 months, the grossest of slander." The large dailies, however, and the political opposition, looked beyond the *Saturday Tribune*'s front pages or its editor's troubled spleen. The *Sun* gloomily contemplated the public's need for a victim and thought that Mr. Jackson's actions, likely approved by Manson, smacked of "the Spanish Inquisition and the beastly Borgias," while the *Province* found fault with the police system and the entire administration of justice in British Columbia. "The abduction cases and the Janet Smith developments out of which they grew," an editorial ran, "provide together a sad commentary on the police system in Greater Vancouver and on the administration of justice in this province. They give evidence first, of an extreme laxity in method, then of a weak yielding to public clamour, and finally of an ignorance or an indifference to some of the principles which lie at the very basis of British justice. Two of these cardinal principles provide that no subject of the King should be arrested or imprisoned except by due process of law, and that a person accused of a crime shall be regarded innocent until he is proven guilty. . . . The thing the citizens have to worry about is the fact that our officers of the peace and officials sworn to enforce the law in British Columbia, could allow themselves to stand idly by while the law was being brought into contempt by methods absolutely at variance with those long established in British countries, and all through a mistaken idea that the public demand for a victim should be satisfied. It is this sort of winking at infractions of the law, this readiness to still public clamour at the expense of justice which has given lynching its hold in the United States, and has made the enforcement of law the overwhelming problem in the American Republic." Speaking for the opposition in the Legislature, C. F. Davie stated that if the archives of every justice department in the Empire were searched, no "such remarkable, astounding and staggering procedures could be found in the annals of criminal justice as has shocked the conscience of the people in connection with this case."

While the opposition sniped and the court debris piled up, or was shovelled away, one small matter passed barely noticed: the hearing, by a grand jury in early October, of a charge of murder of Janet Smith laid against Wong Foon Sing. Busy, week after week, repeating his dismal story of the kidnapping, Wong abstained, on his lawyer's advice, from attendance at his own hearing. The jurors did not need him. After hearing fourteen witnesses, they concluded that "there was no evidence to show a crime had been committed" and "no evidence connecting Wong Foon Sing with a crime."

Wong Foon Sing was free at last to resume his dishonored vocation as Shaughnessy houseboy, or to return to China, from whence he came. He chose the latter. Before departing in early March, he checked with his lawyer, Mr. Senkler, who informed the attorney general's department of his client's intentions and conveyed his willingness to remain if further court action was contemplated. The attorney general replied there was no need for him to stay and in early March Wong sailed off on the *Empress of Russia.* No Jericho Beach seaplanes, Victoria special investigators — or Viennese criminologists — were sent after him.[3]

---

3. According to the *Sun,* November 3, 1928, a visiting Viennese criminologist employed to work in Winnipeg on the case of the disappearance of a five-year-old child stated he intended to visit Vancouver, where "certain persons" wanted him to give his attention to "the unsolved case there several years ago involving Janet Smith, a young Scotch domestic."

END NOTES

1. HIS LORDSHIP

The papers of Alexander Morris, Lieutenant Governor's collection, Public Archives of Manitoba, are a rich source of data on Gordon. *The Manitoban, Manitoba Free Press, Minneapolis Journal,* and *New York Times* carried accounts of His Lordship's doings. W. A. Croffut, "Lord Gordon Gordon, A Bogus Peer and His Distinguished Dupes," *Putnam's Magazine,* January, 1910, and W. W. Folwell, *History of Minnesota* (Saint Paul: Minnesota Historical Society, 1921-1930), vol. 2, app. 5, are informative about Gordon's American interlude. Gordon's New York adversary, Jay Gould, is well described in Gustavus Myers, *History of the Great American Fortunes* (New York: Modern Library, 1936) and E. S. Mott, *Between the Ocean and the Lakes: The Story of Erie* (New York: J. S. Collins, 1899). Useful data on early Manitoba and His Lordship's experiences there can be found in Jeff Gee, *A Sketch of Both Sides of Manitoba* (Nelsonville, Manitoba: Mountainer Book and Job Printers, 1881), George Ham, *Reminiscences of a Raconteur* (Toronto: Musson, 1921), Alexander Begg, *Ten Years in Winnipeg* (Winnipeg: Times Publishers, 1879), Dale and Lee Gibson, *Substantial Justice* (Winnipeg: Peguis Publishers, 1972).

2. DEAD END

The Chilcotin uprising is the subject of Mel Rothenburger's useful *The Chilcotin War* (Langley: Mr. Paperback, 1978). E. S. Hewlett, "The Chilcotin Uprising, a study of Indian-White Relations in 19th Century British Columbia" (M.A. thesis, University of British Columbia, 1972) is a well-researched treatment of the subject. His work is summarized in E. S. Hewlett, "The Chilcotin Uprising of 1864," *B.C. Studies,* no. 19 (Autumn, 1873). *The R. L. Reid Papers,* subject file, Alfred Waddington, Special Collections, University of British Columbia, contains valuable data on the chase, capture, and trial of the Chilcotin fugitives. R. C. Lundin Brown, "Klatsassan, a True Story of Colonial and Military Life," serialized in the *People's Magazine,* 1872, is a detailed account written by the Reverend, who ministered to the condemned Indians. The *Daily British Colonist, British Columbian,* and *Victoria Daily Chronicle* all carried dispatches on the Chilcotin war. F. J. Saunders, " 'Homatcho', or, The Story of the Bute Inlet Expedition and the Massacre by the Chilcotin Indians," *Resources of British Columbia* (March, April 1885) contains first-hand impressions of the Chilcotins. Waddington's career is outlined in Derek Pethik, *Men of British*

Columbia (Saanichton: Hancock House, 1975) and Neville Shanks, *Waddington* (Port Hardy: North Island Gazette Ltd., 1975). David R. Williams, *The Man for a New Country: Sir Matthew Baillie Begbie* (Sidney, B.C.: Gray's Publishing Company, 1977) deals competently with Begbie's career and role in the trial of the fugitives. Useful background data can be found in A. G. Morice, *The History of the Northern Interior of British Columbia* (Fairfield, Washington: Ye Galleon Press, 1971), F. W. Howay, *British Columbia: From the Earliest Times to the Present* (Vancouver: S. J. Clarke, 1914), vol. 2, Cliff Kopas, *Bella Coola* (Vancouver: Mitchell Press, 1970), G. P. V. Akrigg and Helen B. Akrigg, *British Columbia Chronicle 1847-1871* (Vancouver: Discovery Press, 1977).

3. THE SAGA OF RED RYAN

Ryan's criminal record and newspaper clippings on his career are available in the Museum of the Metropolitan Toronto Board of Commissioners of Police, Toronto. Norman J. Ryan's *Red Ryan's Rhymes and Episodes* (Hamilton: Dodge Publications, 1924) is an informative, autobiographical account of Red's early career. The *R. B. Bennett Papers*, Public Archives of Canada, include interesting correspondence relating to Ryan's career and release. Conditions in the Kingston Penitentiary around the time of Red's early residency there are described in *Report of the Royal Commission on Penitentiaries*, Sessional Papers, no. 252 (Ottawa: King's Printer, 1914). J. A. Edmison, "Parole Failures and Parole Successes," *Chitty's Law Journal* (June, 1966) gives some consideration to the Ryan case. In his *Shackling the Transgressor* (Toronto: Thomas Nelson, 1933), Dr. O. J. C. Withrow, who served time with Ryan in the Kingston Penitentiary, describes penitentiary conditions and gives his impressions of Ryan. Another of Ryan's fellow inmates, the Communist party leader, Tim Buck, revealed his own impressions of Ryan and the penitentiary in portions of his *Yours in the Struggle: Reminiscences of Tim Buck*, ed. William Beeching and Phyllis Clarke (Toronto: NC Press, 1977). Ted Honderich, "Why Red Ryan's Shadow Still Hangs Over Every Prison Yard," *Maclean's Magazine*, December 7, 1957, is a useful summary of Ryan's career. The *Toronto Daily Star, Toronto Globe*, and *Toronto Telegram* covered the events, high and low, of Red's career.

4. HOT CARGO

Information on Indian immigration problems and politics in Canada is available in the *H. H. Stevens Papers*, Vancouver City Archives; files of the immigration branch, Department of the Interior, Public Archives of Canada; proceedings of the trial of Bela Singh in *Attorney General of British Columbia Papers*, Public Archives of British Columbia. Kushwant Singh, *The Sikhs Today* (Bombay: Orient Longmans, 1964) surveys Sikh habits, religion, and customs. An excellent overview of Sikh immigration politics in Canada is provided in T. G. Fraser, "The Sikh Problem in Canada and its Political Consequences, 1905-1921," *Journal of Imperial and Commonwealth History*, vol. 7 (October, 1978). R. J. Das, *Hindustani Workers on the Pacific Coast* (Berlin and Leipzig: Walter De Gruyter, 1923) is informative on the economic background of the East

Indians in North America, while Brij Lal "East Indian in British Columbia, 1904-1914, an historical study in growth and integration" (M.A. thesis, University of British Columbia, 1976) is a useful general summary of the British Columbia East Indian community preceding World War I. W. P. Ward, *White Canada Forever* (Montreal: McGill-Queens Press, 1978) treats racism in British Columbia and includes a useful discussion of East Indians. The *Ghadar* and Indian nationalist politics at home and abroad are outlined in Kushwant Singh and Satindra Singh, *Ghadar 1915* (New Delhi: R. and K. Publishing Company, 1966), N. N. Bhattacharya, "Indian Revolutionaries Abroad, 1891-1919," *Journal of Indian History*, vol. 50 (1972), R. C. Majumdar, *History of Freedom Movement in India* (Calcutta: K. L. Mukhopadhyay, 1975), vol. 3. Information of the *Komagata Maru* incident can be found in Sohan Singh Josh, *Tragedy of Komagata Maru* (New Delhi: People's Publishing House, 1975); Hugh Johnston, *The Voyage of the Komagata Maru* (Delhi: Oxford University Press, 1979); Ted Ferguson, *A White Man's Country* (Garden City, N.Y.: Doubleday, 1975); Eric W. Morse, "Some Aspects of the Komagata Maru Affair, 1914," *Report of the Canadian Historical Association* (1936); Robie L. Reid, "The Inside Story of the Komagata Maru," *British Columbia Historical Quarterly*, vol. 5, no. 1 (January, 1941). The *Vancouver Sun, Vancouver Daily Province, Victoria Daily Colonist* are filled with accounts of East Indian immigrant politics in British Columbia.

5. THE ARCTIC CIRCLE WAR

A detailed account of the pursuit of the Mad Trapper can be found in Canada, *Report of the Royal Canadian Mounted Police for the Year Ended September 30, 1932* (Ottawa: King's Printer, 1933). Worthwhile discussions are contained in R. C. Fetherstonhough, *The Royal Canadian Mounted Police* (New York: Carrick and Evans, 1938); Alan Phillips, "Who was the Mad Trapper of Rat River?" *Maclean's Magazine*, October 1, 1955; T. E. G. Shaw, "Manhunt in the Arctic," *R.C.M.P. Quarterly*, vol. 26, no. 2 (1960). Dick North, *The Mad Trapper of Rat River* (Toronto: Macmillan, 1972) is devoted to a full and fair rendering of the Johnson affair. The *Edmonton Bulletin, Edmonton Free Press, Winnipeg Free Press,* and *Toronto Globe* carried numerous reports of the search, chase, and death of Albert Johnson.

6. THE HOUSEBOY

The bulk of the material of the Janet Smith story is drawn from reports of inquests, trials, and investigations in the British Columbia daily metropolitan press: *Vancouver Evening Sun, Vancouver Daily Province, Victoria Daily Colonist,* and *Victoria Daily Times.* James Morton, *In the Sea of Sterile Mountains* (Vancouver: J. J. Douglas, 1974) provides some background material on anti-orientalism in the 1920s in British Columbia. A useful summary of the Janet Smith case is included in Eric Nicol, *Vancouver* (Toronto: Doubleday, 1970). The *Attorney-General Papers*, Public Archives of British Columbia, contains brief summaries of the conclusion of the coroner's inquests of July and September, 1924.

INDEX

155

ABOUT THE AUTHOR

Born in Winnipeg, Manitoba, Martin Robin currently teaches in the Department of Political Science at Simon Fraser University. Known to many as the author of the best seller *The Bad and the Lonely*, his writing credits include several books about Canadian politics and articles contributed to many periodicals, including *Canadian Dimension, Canadian Historical Review*, and *Canadian Forum*. In addition, he has written, narrated, and edited numerous political and social documentaries for CBC radio and television.

Martin Robin lives in Burnaby, British Columbia, with his wife, Grace, and their three daughters.